£10

Tristernagh Priory, County Westmeath

Maynooth Studies in Local History

SERIES EDITOR Raymond Gillespie

This volume is one of six short books published in the Maynooth Studies in Local History series in 2018. Like their predecessors they range widely, both chronologically and geographically, over the local experience in the Irish past. Chronologically they span the worlds of medieval Tristernagh in Westmeath, a study of an early 19th-century land improver, the Famine of the 1840s in Kinsale, politics and emigration in the late 19th century and sectarian rituals in the late 19th and 20th centuries. Geographically they range across the length of the country from Derry to Kinsale and westwards from Westmeath to Galway. Socially they move from those living on the margins of society in Kinsale and Galway in the middle of the 19th century to the politics and economics of the middle class revealed in the world of Thomas Bermingham and the splits in Westmeath in the 1890s. In doing so they reveal diverse and complicated societies that created the local past, and present the range of possibilities open to anyone interested in studying that past. Those possibilities involve the dissection of the local experience in the complex and contested social worlds of which it is part as people strove to preserve and enhance their positions within their local societies. Such studies of local worlds over such long periods are vital for the future since they not only stretch the historical imagination but provide a longer perspective on the shaping of society in Ireland, helping us to understand the complex evolution of the Irish experience. These works do not simply chronicle events relating to an area within administrative or geographically determined boundaries, but open the possibility of understanding how and why particular regions had their own personality in the past. Such an exercise is clearly one of the most exciting challenges for the future and demonstrates the vitality of the study of local history in Ireland.

Like their predecessors, these six short books are reconstructions of the socially diverse worlds of the poor as well as the rich, women as well as men, the geographical marginal as well as those located near the centre of power. They reconstruct the way in which those who inhabited those worlds lived their daily lives, often little affected by the large themes that dominate the writing of national history. They also provide models that others can follow up and adapt in their own studies of the Irish past. In such ways will we understand better the regional diversity of Ireland and the social and cultural basis for that diversity. They, with their predecessors, convey the vibrancy and excitement of the world of Irish local history today.

Maynooth Studies in Local History: Number 137

Tristernagh Priory, County Westmeath
Colonial monasticism in medieval Ireland

Tadhg O'Keeffe

FOUR COURTS PRESS

Set in 10pt on 12pt Bembo by
Carrigboy Typesetting Services for
FOUR COURTS PRESS LTD
7 Malpas Street, Dublin 8, Ireland
www.fourcourtspress.ie
and in North America for
FOUR COURTS PRESS
c/o IPG, 814 N Franklin St, Chicago, IL 60622

ISBN 978–1–84682–718–1

Printed in Ireland
by SprintPrint, Dublin.

Contents

Introduction

L ittle remains of the priory of Tristernagh, Co. Westmeath, founded around the year 1200 for Augustinian canons regular and dedicated to the Blessed Virgin Mary. Its domestic buildings were replaced with new residential and service structures in the centuries after its dissolution in 1536, but its church remained largely intact until 1783 when Sir Pigott William Piers, the landlord who owned the site and its associated land, embarked on a programme of demolition. Although some medieval fabric survived, an important link with the world of the Middle Ages was severed. The Piers family, which had already owned Tristernagh for almost two-and-a-half centuries, did not enjoy much prosperity on the old medieval estate after the priory's destruction, and tradition has it that ill-fortune was their reward for interfering with the ancient inheritance. Maria Edgeworth's *Castle Rackrent* was reputedly based on the family and its mansion on the site, Tristernagh House, which suggests that there was already mismanagement of the estate before 1800. In the early 19th century, the Piers family lost possession and Tristernagh eventually ended up being sold off as an encumbered estate.

Tristernagh Priory had enjoyed a central role in the life of the Irish midlands for centuries (fig. 1). It had been founded by Geoffrey de Costentin, whose father had been involved in the Anglo-Norman invasion of Ireland a few decades earlier. Although an ecclesiastical institution, its foundation was part of Geoffrey's strategy to control and settle with fellow Anglo-Normans the district to the north-west of Mullingar. It was, in every respect, a colonial establishment. Its early charters were witnessed by senior ecclesiastics who had been born in England and had come to Ireland during the invasion, and its architecture was English in style. In more than 300 years of operation it had only one prior of Irish descent.

Located deep within a large estate and endowed with various rights and resources from the outset, Tristernagh functioned as a fairly self-contained and independent economic unit. Its own farmland circled it on three sides, and it owned most of the resources of the lake – Lough Iron – which flanked it on the other side. Grants of other resources from benefactors during the 13th century enhanced its prosperity. Although it was rural, it was not isolated. About three kilometres to its west was the small town of Kilbixy. Indeed, the priory was often referred to in the Middle Ages as the priory of Kilbixy. This town was established by Geoffrey around the time that he founded the priory, and it was populated at the outset with Anglo-Norman settlers. In common with many

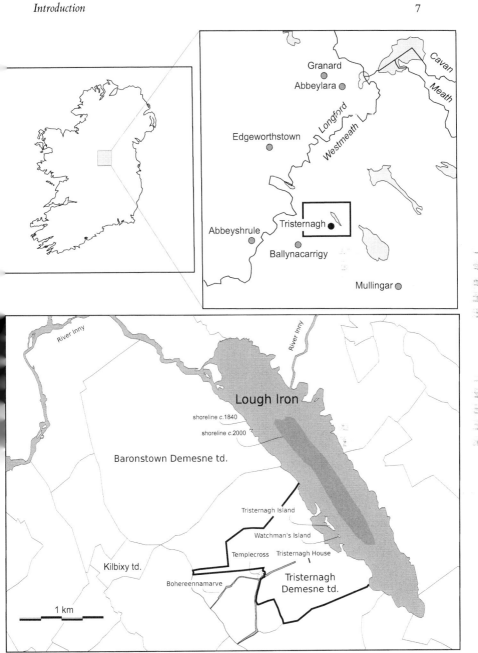

1. Location of Tristernagh Priory.

of the invaders' new nucleated settlements, Kilbixy had been a place of some importance in the period before the invasion. As a market centre, it helped the new priory and its community get access to the regional economy, and as a place with an Anglo-Norman castle – one was erected in 1192 – it offered security to the district.

Priory and town prospered in tandem for some centuries, aided by their distance from competing monasteries and urban settlements, and protected by a ring of castles built by various Anglo-Normans. But the prosperity did not last. The town depopulated at some unknown date later in the Middle Ages – it disappears from the sources before 1500 – while the priory was abandoned and its last few residents were pensioned off in 1536. The Piers landlords of the 18th century, fixated on both the improvement of their land and the display of their own wealth, draped a new landscape across the old, disguising or, in the priory's case, largely destroying most of the vestiges of the medieval past. The casual visitor today to the rural townlands between the small village of Ballynacarrigy and the now-shrinking Lough Iron to its north-east could be forgiven, then, for thinking that the area was relatively unimportant in the Middle Ages. The 1192 motte-and-bailey castle and the earthworks on the site of the medieval town might catch his or her eye, but the fragmentary remains of the priory are well off the beaten track. A signpost on a minor road directs the visitor to a long cul-de-sac which terminates at rusting gates set into collapsing later 18th-century piers. The ruin stands unenticingly in the distance, isolated on private land that is boggy underfoot and criss-crossed by electric fences (fig. 2).

Contemporary documentation for the district during the Middle Ages is variable in quality. It leaves unanswered many questions about the settlement in Kilbixy in particular, in part because it is an ambiguous record but mainly because it is simply an incomplete record. Was its castle built by Geoffrey de Costentin? When was the settlement given a charter by which it enjoyed borough status? How many people lived in the town and where exactly did they come from? Were people of native descent ever allowed to reside as burgesses, and, if so, from what date? When and why was the settlement eventually abandoned? Some of the many questions that one can ask might one day be answered in archaeological investigations, but most of the issues will never be resolved: the answers are not in the ground, and any documents which contained the answers are long destroyed.

The documentary record for Tristernagh is significantly better. The priory and some of its personnel appear in a wide range of sources but the key source is a 14th-century register containing copies of charters pertaining to the priory, mainly in the period to *c*.1235.[1] This register provides essential information on the priory's possessions, as well as plenty of ancillary information, including the names of individuals who made or witnessed transactions in its favour. It is divided into two parts, the first containing general grants, including two 'foundation charters', and the second containing a general statement of the

2. The only surviving fragment of Tristernagh Priory viewed through the gateway into the estate of the former Piers family residence; the only surviving 18th-century building is visible to the right through the bars of the gate.

liberties of the priory followed by assorted charters and records of grants as well as of papal and episcopal confirmations. Yet, as with the secular settlement at Kilbixy, there are many questions that are not answered directly in Tristernagh's documentary record. When exactly was the priory founded? Why was it founded several miles from Kilbixy, rather than in or beside the settlement itself? Why did Geoffrey de Costentin establish it for Augustinians and not – the other option – Cistercians? Did its canons follow any particular Augustinian observance? Where did these canons come from? Where had the masons who built it worked previously? These questions all pertain to the early history of the priory, the main focus of this book.

Few monastic registers survive from medieval Ireland. How did this one manage to do so? It seems to have remained in the area after the dissolution, and probably even on the premises. Edmund Nugent, the bishop of Kilmore who administered Tristernagh late in its history as an ecclesiastical establishment, was allowed to keep the goods of the priory in order to pay off the priory's debts.[2] Although of no great monetary value in itself, the register was probably among those goods. There is circumstantial evidence that it had ended up in the library of the original, post-dissolution, Tristernagh House by at least the early 17th century. First, the Piers family, possessors of the property from 1562, knew where it was at that time and had access to it: a copy was made under commission by one Christopher Fitzgerald of Laragh in 1618. Second, Sir James Ware, the great antiquarian whose eldest daughter, Martha, married into the Piers family, possessed the original at one stage, and the fact that he also owned the Fitzgerald copy – it ended up among his papers in the Bodleian Library, Oxford (MS Rawlinson B 504) – suggests that he acquired the original at Tristernagh itself. Whatever the case, the original was in Tristernagh in 1716 when the 3rd Baronet, Sir Henry Piers, had it rebound along with a new transcription and translation by Daniel Egan. Its whereabouts thereafter is unknown but Walter Harris, the antiquarian and husband of Ware's granddaughter, was able to access it because he annotated it when revising Ware's work on Irish bishops. By 1758 it had passed, through an unrecorded transaction, into the possession of one Michael Ignatius Dugan, who probably sold it to John Lodge, from whose collection it ended up in the library of Armagh Cathedral.[3]

A Latin transcription of the manuscript by Maud Violet Clarke, who had substituted for F.M. Powicke as professor of history at Queen's University, Belfast, between 1916 and 1919, was published under the imprint of the Irish Manuscripts Commission in 1941.[4] She died six years before it was published, leaving the final stage of work to two of her former students, J.S.A. Macauley and K.M.E. Murray. The former was responsible for the important task of collating Clarke's transcription of the manuscript with the two earlier transcriptions, by Fitzgerald and Egan in 1618 and 1716 respectively. This collation was necessary because the original manuscript had deteriorated since those copies were made. Murray was responsible for writing a brief history of the de Costentin family, for summarizing the priory's medieval history based on the content of the register, and for accounting for its post-dissolution history. Forty years later, Elizabeth Hickey, in a paper that unfortunately is poorly referenced, revisited the priory's post-medieval history, glossing Murray's account of the Piers family, Tristernagh's eventual owners, with further information.[5] In 1989, Brian Eager published a summary of the priory in the Middle Ages, drawing entirely on the register, and he emphasized its function as an agent of colonization.[6] Since then, little has been written about the priory and its environs. Pride of place among the few exceptions must go to a comprehensive history of the locality by Peter Wallace and others in 2014.[7]

Is there a need for a new study of the priory and its estate? Would a translation of the register from the Latin into English not be a more useful publication? To address the second question first, a translation of the published transcription would certainly allow the register reach a much wider readership than the 1941 volume, and that readership would find intrinsically interesting the manner in which the charters detail what is being granted, under what conditions, and to whom, and so on.[8] So, it would be a very useful project, though probably better suited to online than print publication. It would probably require a revisiting of the original manuscript material and probably also a revision of the collation of texts by Macauley. In answer to the first question – do we need a new study? – there is certainly value in simply revisiting the priory, armed with the richer insights made possible by recent research into medieval Ireland, its monasteries, and the buildings and lands of those monasteries. Such a revisiting not only allows a more comprehensive contextual understanding of Tristernagh and its locality, but makes a wider contribution to local history studies in general by using the priory to explain aspects of medieval ecclesiastical organization, land-holding and architecture, and to demonstrate the use of sources of varying kinds. This short book was written in that spirit.

My account of Tristernagh cannot be the last word on any aspect of the priory's history. There is much in the register that would require far more space than is available here, and there are also records of the priory through the late Middle Ages, the period that is not covered in the register. In any case, a definitive study of the priory would require collaboration between scholars from different fields. My contribution in this short book to the larger project of understanding Tristernagh is to shine a light on a key source for its early history which has long been known but never interrogated: the set of drawings of the demolished priory church – two views and a ground plan – which were made by Angelo Mario Bigari and Gabriel Beranger when they visited Tristernagh in 1779.

Why are these drawings important to the medieval historian? After all, they were made long after the priory was dissolved. First, they tell us much about the history of the church as a structure in and of itself in the Middle Ages. That history matters because the church was the focal building of the priory: generations of canons had their lives organized around the times that they were required to spend within it, while secular individuals of means such as Geoffrey de Costentin invested in its construction and upkeep, and desired to be buried inside it. Second, through comparative architectural-historical analysis based on the drawings, the church can be placed within contemporary, overlapping, worlds of ideas – local, regional, international – about style, the political motivations of medieval style choices, and the ways in which style expressed identity in the Middle Ages. If documentary sources allow us to reconstruct Tristernagh's history from records of activities and events, comparative analysis of the architectural evidence as recorded by Bigari and Beranger allows us to fill out that history with insights into the cultural world of the people who shaped the priory through patronage or craftsmanship.

In giving these late 18th-century drawings such prominence in this study, I also want to show how the historian, 'local' or not, can read history from stone or, where the stone is gone, from reliable antiquarian drawings. Specialist knowledge is needed to derive the full benefit of the architectural-historical record, but the non-specialist can achieve much by simply looking at that

3. Map of sites mentioned in the text; see also figs 1, 9, 15.

record and making observations based on a small amount of knowledge and
common sense. The documentary historian can also learn how to decipher
historic architecture from reading the work of the architectural historian and by
observing the language and construction of architectural-historical arguments.[9]
Therefore, I deliberately explain here how I arrived at conclusions about the

priory's architecture, rather than simply report those conclusions. While the focus of this study is a medieval ecclesiastical building, the approach used here is applicable to historic buildings regardless of function or date: one determines whether a building has one phase or many phases of construction, one looks for parallels to determine the features which are typical or unique, and one evaluates the relevance of all that information in the context of the history being assembled from more conventional (documentary) sources.

The locations of places mentioned in this book are shown in fig. 3, p. 12.

1. The de Costentin family and Kilbixy

Hugh de Lacy accompanied Henry II on his first visit to Ireland in 1171. The following year he was granted overlordship of the vast territory that made up the ancient kingdom of Mide. The new lordship extended wedge-like from east to west, from a short littoral centred on the town of Drogheda towards the Shannon. It enveloped all of the lands now contained within counties Meath and Westmeath, as well as most of Longford and, thanks to some further expansion by Hugh's son Walter, parts of what is now south Ulster. Hugh explored his new territory in 1172, zig-zaging his way into the lakelands of Westmeath before turning back towards the place where he had decided to establish his capital, Trim. He probably had very little knowledge of the land to the west of Fore.[1]

Following the conventional medieval practice, Hugh subdivided the lordship into smaller land units and granted them to his followers to hold as his tenants. The *chanson de geste* which is popularly known as *The song of Dermot and the earl*, a contemporary account of the beginnings of Anglo-Norman lordship in Ireland, records these grants and the names of the recipients. Included in the list is a grant of Kilbixy to one Geoffrey de Costentin.[2] In common with the other land grants in Meath, the district assigned to Geoffrey was an existing native Irish political unit: the tuath, originally the kingdom, of Uí Moccu Uais,[3] now represented by the barony of Moygoish (fig. 4). The territory was identified as Kilbixy because its principal church was *Ceall Bhigsighe*, the Church of St Bigseach.

Geoffrey, scion of a family that originated in the Cotentin region of Normandy, probably came to Ireland from Lincolnshire, where a minor branch of the de Costentin family held land.[4] The date of his arrival is uncertain but he was on the island by at least 1176, judging by the date of a charter which he witnessed in respect of St Mary's Abbey in Dublin.[5] While it is conceivable that he travelled to Ireland in the company of some other individuals with Lincolnshire connections who took land granted to them by Hugh in the western part of the lordship,[6] it is apparent that Geoffrey did not settle alongside them in Meath. From c.1176 until his death, probably in 1181, he was in Laigis (Laois), courtesy of a grant from Richard de Clare (Strongbow).[7] If Hugh wanted a tenant to occupy and settle quickly the frontier lands west of Lough Iron in the mid-1170s, Geoffrey was not available. Hugh was not deterred by

4. Map of the barony of Moygoish, Co. Westmeath. The parish boundaries are those marked on the mid-17th-century Down Survey.

5. The late 12th-century donjon ('keep') on the Rock of Dunamase.

the inability of some grantees to take up the land he intended for them: Meiler fitzHenry was also granted land in Meath and he, too, was in Leinster. Even if some of the grants were fundamentally speculative, Hugh had a clear strategy in allocating parts of his new lordship to individuals, and he took the path of least resistance in determining that their boundaries be defined by those of existing tuatha. Kilbixy saw no permanent Anglo-Norman presence during Hugh's lifetime but the grant to Geoffrey de Costentin was never retracted. The de Costentin family did eventually take it up.

Geoffrey was not a minor figure in the affairs of Anglo-Norman Leinster. Goddard Orpen believed that Strongbow built a castle within the ancient *dún* of Dunamase in Laois between 1173 and 1175, and that he may have appointed Geoffrey to be its custodian.[8] The first stone fortifications on the summit of the Rock of Dunamase were probably built under Geoffrey's supervision (fig. 5).[9] In 1177 he was among the witnesses to the charter by which the priory of St Thomas the Martyr in Dublin was founded.[10] A (now unidentified) place named Drum Costentin in the barony of Forth (Carlow) was granted (before 1185) to the priory of St Thomas the Martyr in Dublin,[11] which is further evidence that he was in Leinster during the formative years of Hugh de Lacy's lordship of Meath.

LAOIS, MEATH AND THE YOUNGER GEOFFREY

Gerald of Wales recorded that in 1181 Meiler fitzHenry, an accomplished soldier, was granted on behalf of the king 'the province of Laois', described as 'a hostile, difficult and wooded region', in lieu of lands in Kildare which had previously been ear-marked for him.[12] It was a strategic transfer orchestrated by agents of the king – they 'assigned this remote border area to a borderer' – and Gerald made no reference to any de Costentin. It is likely that Geoffrey had died in 1181 and that the transfer followed his death.[13] Geoffrey's son, also Geoffrey, might have been regarded as too inexperienced for the task. He might also have been too young: his date of birth is not recorded, but he died in 1232[14] having enjoyed a distinguished career over the previous three decades, so he was probably a minor in the 1180s.

The date at which the de Costentins first arrived in Meath is not recorded. The earliest possible date is 1181. It is conceivable that the grant of Laois to Meiler and the relocation of the major branch of the de Costentins to the allocated territory in the de Lacy lordship – another branch remained in Laois[15] – were near-simultaneous events. It might not be insignificant that in that year de Lacy gave to Meiler the hand of his niece in marriage, and that he simultaneously built a castle for him in Timahoe in Laois.[16]

There is, however, a stronger case for a date more than a decade later. There is ample evidence that the subinfeudation of Meath was incomplete 'on the ground' by the time of Hugh's death in 1186, with many lands in the western part of the lordship still to see a significant Anglo-Norman presence. No English bishop had yet been appointed to either of the two dioceses, Ardagh and Clonard/Meath, which claimed, or were soon to claim, jurisdiction over the churches in western Meath. The slow pace of settlement there is further indicated by the fact that as late as 1216 the diocese of Meath had five rural deaneries, all in the east of the lordship (Dunshaughlin, Kells, Skreen, Slane and Trim).[17]

Hugh's son, Walter, was still a minor in 1186, so Meath entered a period of wardship. John, Henry II's youngest son and lord of Ireland, identified Walter's minority as an opportunity to grab land within the lordship, and he built some castles as a strategy to alienate barely settled land that rightfully belonged to the de Lacys.[18] Although his role is not recorded, he must have been responsible for the castle built at Kilbixy in 1192.[19] The lordship of Meath was restored to Walter in 1194 on the payment of a fine of 2,500 marks to John. Either in gratitude or as part of the restoration agreement, Walter acceded in 1195 to a petition from John in confirming a grant to Geoffrey, all for the service of four knights, of five fees in Moygoish, along with the castle in Kilbixy, and fifteen fees in the adjoining territory of Conmaicne.[20] The original de Lacy grant, recorded in *The song*, had not included Conmaicne, most of it in Co. Longford and roughly coterminous with the diocese of Ardagh.[21] This petition strongly suggests that the de Costentin family only entered the Kilbixy area in the early 1190s, and that John had orchestrated the move from Leinster.[22]

Who were these knights and what were these 'fees'? A fee, or fief, was the land granted to a lord to support a knight who would provide military service to the grantor in return. The principle was simple; the reality was complex. First, the fee was not a land-unit of fixed metrical size, even though there were often attempts at metrical consistency. It was not uncommon for fiefs to be constituted of carucates (ploughlands, of 120 acres) in multiples of five, thus giving an average knight's fee in Dublin an area of 10 carucates and its equivalent in Meath an average of 20 carucates, for example, but local circumstances and conditions often militated against exact fits;[23] the canons of Tristernagh, as will be shown below, had some grants of land that were measured in multiples of five carucates. Second, not every fief had a knight: an individual knight could have land in several fees, so the military return from certain blocks of land was often calculated as a fraction of a fee; thus, for example, lands could be assessed as ½ a knight's fee or an even smaller fraction. Third, those armed men (or *miles*) who were assigned land were not necessarily the chivalric knights of popular imagination but could be 'all grades from substantial landowners to men who had to be content with a small holding that put them on a level with the … peasant'.[24] In the 11th and 12th centuries in Europe soldiers with clearly defined fees had an expectation of seeing some action in the field, or at least some period of castle-guard (serving in the garrison of a castle for a specific duration, in other words). However, those 'fractional knights' – those who held land of various lords in various places – probably escaped such obligations because the service that could be expected of them was itself fragmented. The Anglo-Normans introduced the concept of knight service to Ireland, but from at least the early 13th century lords in Ireland could render scutage, a money payment, in lieu of providing knights.[25] Scutage was especially appropriate in places like Westmeath: it was better to keep armed men in such localities if possible than have them march off to other locations for the customary period of 40 days.

We cannot identify the men who were, at least in theory, to provide the military service to Walter de Lacy from the de Costentin estate, but we can see that the organization of Moygoish and Conmaicne in 1195 followed the familiar pattern in the feudal world, with 20 fees between them. The normal quota of knights to be provided to the feudal host from the discrete territorial unit held by an individual tenant-in-chief was either five or a multiple of five,[26] so Moygoish was a standard feudal holding while Conmaicne was three times the size of one. These territories were not returning the requisite number of knights – there was only one knight for every five fees – but clearly the intention was that Geoffrey would attract the men who could then render military service. The breakdown of the fees suggests that the geography of Moygoish was already known. Conmaice, by contrast, was less well-defined (although it did extend as far south as Lough Iron).[27]

THE SETTLEMENT AT KILBIXY

As the *caput* of Moygoish, Kilbixy was relatively secure in 1195. Geoffrey had custody of the 1192 castle. It can be identified as the motte-and-bailey in the townland of Baronstown Demesne (fig. 6). Close examination of this monument reveals some interesting things. The motte is circular in plan, with a diameter of about 30m and a height of about 11m, and is surrounded by a fosse and outer bank. The spatial relationship of the mound to the enclosing fosse and bank – it is very slightly off-centre – would suggest that the monument was originally a ringfort and that it was converted into an Anglo-Norman castle in 1192 by the insertion of the mound into its centre. The summit of the motte was enclosed at an unknown (but presumably early) date by a wall, low foundations of which remain. Within the summit enclosure are fragmentary, grassed-over, remains of two small buildings, one square and one rectangular. In the absence of excavation, the two structures might be interpreted as the remains of an Anglo-Norman tower-and-hall pair, similar to but much smaller than the pair found on the summit of Clough Castle, Co. Down. The square building at Kilbixy could only have been a two-storey tower with a very small upper chamber for the lord, while the rectangular building is best interpreted as the remains of a very tiny hall – basically a small rectangular room – just about big enough for an audience with a lord.[28] These structures were not intended for long-term use.

6. Kilbixy motte from the north-west.

There is a small embanked bailey on the south-west side of the mound, and it appears secondary to the fosse around the mound.

The 1195 petition makes no reference to a settlement at Kilbixy, but that should not surprise us. The castle was effectively a beach-head, a point of fortification without which settlers would not be tempted to gravitate to the area. The task of bringing in settlers would have been left to Geoffrey. A considerable amount of progress was made very quickly after 1195. Tristernagh's 'foundation charters', discussed below, name a number of individuals who, by the first decade of the 13th century, had lands around Kilbixy which were measured in carucates or half-carucates. These were people whom Geoffrey had settled in the area; we know this because he exercised the authority to grant parts of their lands to the canons of Tristernagh in exchange for lands elsewhere.

Burgage land is mentioned in one of the 'foundation charters',[29] indicating that the Kilbixy settlement had borough status early in the 13th century. Little is known otherwise of its earliest history. One Eadric the weaver – his name suggests he was of Anglo-Saxon descent – is recorded in one of the charters as having had a toft in the vill of Kilbixy;[30] was he a first-generation burgess, and where did he go? Those settlers around Kilbixy whose names are recorded in the 'foundation charters' are likely also to have held property in the settlement by burgage tenure.

The promise of such tenure might have been instrumental in the decision of these settlers to move to the area in the first instance. Burgesses – the permanent inhabitants of boroughs – enjoyed greater rights and privileges than their rural counterparts, all in return for the payment of an annual rent (normally one shilling), so Anglo-Norman lords in Ireland, like their counterparts elsewhere, founded boroughs to attract settlers to certain localities.[31] In some instances the status was granted to existing settlements in order to promote their growth into towns, but in others the grant was entirely speculative, the aim being to attract people to relatively empty rural locations where they could then establish settlements. Boroughs were not necessarily towns in a functional sense: the privileges and rights bestowed on burgesses largely pertained to conditions of tenure, and they did not lead automatically to the development of the secondary (manufacturing) or tertiary (service) industries that one associates with urban places. Many boroughs in Anglo-Norman Ireland were rural villages. Robin Glasscock's term 'rural borough'[32] is rarely used by scholars now, but it does actually evoke the character of many medieval boroughs, including Kilbixy.

The site of the settlement itself is marked by one of the most extensive and best preserved systems of earthworks of any deserted medieval settlement in Ireland (fig. 7). The main concentration is in the large field opposite the entrance to the churchyard. Two intersecting roadways can be identified there. One runs away from the churchyard towards the south-west. Most of the identifiable house plots are on the north side of it. The other runs perpendicular to it (and parallel to the modern road) before veering off in the same direction, and there seems to be another roadway leading off it towards the south. At the junction of the two roadways is a raised area of triangular plan, around which runs another roadway or trackway. Inspection of the earthwork traces of house plots within this whole area suggests more than one phase of construction or occupation.

The field to the south-east of the churchyard was identified on the 1st edition OS map (1837) as '*Site of* Kilbixy Town' and given the field name 'Burgess Land'. One cannot say whether the surveyors saw earthworks which are now gone or were informed by locals that it had been the town site.

There are earthworks to the north-east of the churchyard and motte-and-bailey but they are very denuded and one cannot be certain that they represent actual settlement. There is a very obvious hollow-way immediately north-east of the church and castle, and it is parallel to and equidistant from both the modern road (which appears to be on the site of an older road) and another roadway or trackway further to the north-east. The regular spacing of these roadways suggests a very ordered landscape. Were the burgesses allotted land between these lines of communication, and is that why part of the land on the south side of the church was remembered as 'Burgess Land'?

The only medieval building to survive above-ground in the entire settlement area is in the churchyard. In 1489, Archbishop Fleming of Armagh granted an indulgence to those who contributed financially to the leper house of

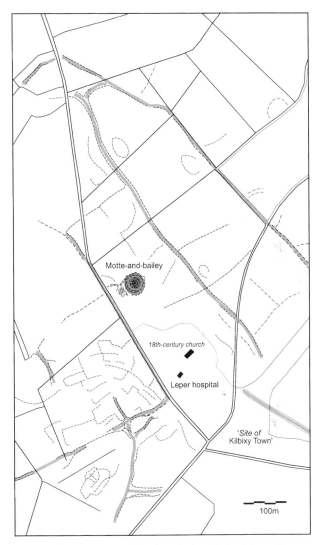

7. A preliminary survey of earthworks (mainly banks) at Kilbixy.
Suggested lines of roads are indicated by light shading.

St Brigid in Kilbixy,[33] and the building in the churchyard has been identified since the mid-19th century as this very foundation.[34] It is marked on the 1st edition OS map as 'Leper hospital or Bridget's hospital' (fig. 8). This is how it was remembered in the locality, so we should give that some credence. It is marked on the 1656 Down Survey map as a small two-storeyed tower (it was actually three storeys high), and it is placed to the east rather than the west of

8. The Kilbixy 'leper hospital' (photo: Peter Wallace).

the church.[35] Aubrey Gwynn and Neville Hadcock attributed its construction to Hugh de Lacy in the incorrect belief that he built the motte and that it and the motte were contemporary.[36] The architecture of the building, insofar as one can see it under ivy, does not indicate so early a date. Also, there is no record of a hospital in Kilbixy in the Tristernagh register.

The site of a castle in the area of the town was noted in 1837 but the site was not recorded on the map.[37] Was this the 'ruinous castle' mentioned in the extent of the priory lands in 1540, and (or?) the 'large piece of an old square castle called the Burgage-castle' that was recorded in 1692?[38] A castle is depicted in Cumminstown townland, west of Kilbixy, on the Down Survey, and its site is marked on the 1st edition OS map.

The new settlement needed a church. The exceptionally fine 18th-century parish church in Kilbixy marks the site of the original *Ceall Bhigsighe*.[39] Comparative evidence from elsewhere in Ireland would indicate that this original site was still in use by the time that the Anglo-Normans arrived in the area but that its first (7th-century?) church had been rebuilt in stone at least once. The first Anglo-Norman communal Mass was celebrated in this building. The invaders were relatively slow to replace existing local churches with new buildings,[40] so one cannot assume that Geoffrey moved quickly to modernize or rebuild the pre-invasion church at Kilbixy as soon as he took up the grant.

A pre-1202 charter in the Tristernagh register[41] confirms that the church in Kilbixy served as the principal church of the de Costentin grant, and was provided with its tithes. This provision allows us to describe it as the

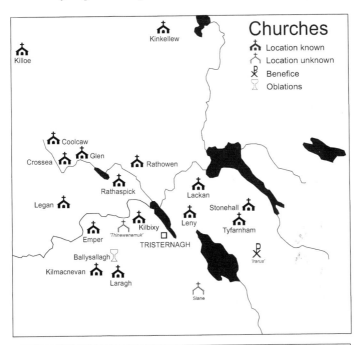

9. Churches and tithes possessed by Tristernagh Priory. The priory also had a church at Keenagh, possibly Clough, Co. Longford, and tithes from Leckintown, Co. Dublin.

parish church. While the church's primacy among places of worship within Anglo-Norman Moygoish was obviously a continuation of the pre-invasion arrangement, it is more difficult to claim that the tithing system in Moygoish was also an inheritance from the pre-invasion period. Opinion is divided as to whether there was tithing, and by extension a system of parishes, in Ireland before the Anglo-Norman arrival.[42] The evidence pertaining to Kilbixy's church offers no support to either argument; it tells us only that the church was parochial before 1202.

In line with the contemporary practice of secular lords in respect of parochial administration, Geoffrey disconnected himself from the administrative and financial affairs of this church. However, rather than grant its advowson (the right to appoint the priest) and impropriation (the destination of the tithes) to a monastic house, as was normal, he granted them to Ralph Petit, the archdeacon of Meath. This is very revealing. There was no lack of monastic houses to which Geoffrey could have gifted Kilbixy. St Thomas's in Dublin, an abbey since 1192 and a foundation much favoured by the de Lacys among others, was an obvious potential recipient. But Geoffrey obviously planned to establish a monastery himself and to have it enriched through tithes from parish churches within his lands. Once Tristernagh Priory was founded, effectively in partnership with Petit, the tithes of the church in Kilbixy were transferred to it, with Petit listed among the witnesses to the transfer.[43] If Simon de Rochfort, the bishop of Meath, exerted any pressure on Geoffrey to donate the church and tithes to St Thomas's, where he had been a prior until 1192, or to his own new cathedral priory of Newtown Trim, there is no record of it. On the contrary, he witnessed those very transactions in favour of Tristernagh. By the early 14th century the priory had churches or chapels across western Meath, as well as the church in Balrothery, Co. Dublin; it also had tithes from several parishes where it seems not to have had the advowson (fig. 9).

The church in Kilbixy remained in use as the parish church through the Middle Ages. There survives in the churchyard a small octagonal baptismal font, dated by Helen Roe to the post-Reformation period.[44] In 1682, Sir Henry Piers described it as 'the remains of an ancient and well built church, the mother of many churches and chapels about it, which had at the west end a very well built high tower or steeple'.[45] The accuracy of his description is confirmed by the illustration of a western tower on the Down Survey map of 1656.[46]

CONCLUSION

Hugh de Lacy's plan to settle the de Costentin family in the western part of the lordship of Meath only came to fruition almost a decade after his death. Anglo-Normans had certainly traversed the district west of Lough Iron between 1172 and 1195, and some of them built a castle at Kilbixy in 1192 following an instruction from the Lord John, but there is no evidence of permanent settlement in the Kilbixy area until the younger Geoffrey de Costentin arrived from Laois in the mid-1190s. It is testimony to the difficulties which Anglo-Norman barons faced in finding properly equipped settlers for frontier regions, but also to the oscillating fortunes of the de Lacy family itself, that the tuath of Uí Moccu Uais had no colonial settlement of substance two decades after Hugh de Lacy had made it the subject of a grant. Geoffrey moved quickly to settle the land once he arrived, starting with the promotion of a new chartered settlement at Kilbixy itself. He began simultaneously the process of securing tithes and other resources for a scheme on which he was to embark shortly after 1200: the foundation of a major new monastic house.

2. The foundation of Tristernagh Priory

Once settled in Kilbixy, Geoffrey enjoyed a profile at least equal to that of his father. As a leading magnate who was achieving some success in settling and making relatively secure his corner of a region that was still identified as a frontier, he was clearly regarded very highly by the king. In 1200 he was assigned the cantred of Tirieghrachbothe, identified by Orpen as *Tír Fhiachrach bhfeadha* (the Faes of Athlone), which he was to hold by the service of five knights,[1] while the adjacent cantred in south Roscommon, Tirmany, *Tír Maine*, was granted to him in 1201.[2] These lands, effectively a buffer zone between Leinster and the Connacht lands which had been granted to William de Burgh but not yet settled by Anglo-Normans,[3] were ostensibly given to him in exchange for the lands in Laois of which he was deprived 19 years earlier. It is possible that the motte at Cloonburren, Co. Roscommon (a little downriver from the royal castle of Clonmacnoise, Co. Offaly), was built under his instruction at this time. Such was his standing in the Irish lordship that he was made deputy governor in 1201–2.[4] When the royal castle of Athlone was rebuilt in 1210 he was appointed its first constable, a position to which he was reappointed in 1215.[5] At this time he was also custodian, on behalf of the king, of the castles of Loxseudy (Ballymore, Co. Westmeath) and Hincheleder (site unknown), which had been confiscated from the de Lacys.[6] In 1215, John took into his own hands the cantred of Tirieghrachbothe and gave Geoffrey instead the cantred of Trithweth to the north-west of Lough Ree for the service of four knights.[7] In 1229, Geoffrey was involved in yet another exchange when the king, now Henry III, took into his own hand the fees in Trithweth, along with those of four other cantreds in Roscommon,[8] and compensated Geoffrey with Connacht lands further away from Athlone and nearer to the Irish.[9] It is probably not insignificant that in the same year, 1229, Geoffrey was pardoned as a reward for his service in Ireland the scutage owed from Thorpe in Staffordshire.[10] The new lands in Roscommon were not settled by Geoffrey, and in any case he was possibly preoccupied with duties in Dublin, having been appointed keeper of the see of Dublin during a vacancy in 1229.[11] We cannot say how much time he spent in Kilbixy during these three decades, but plenty of records indicate that various duties brought him away. He never built a stone castle in Kilbixy. Perhaps he resided in the priory when he was in the area.

THE 'FOUNDATION' CHARTERS

Shortly after his arrival in Meath and with his stock rising, Geoffrey followed through on his plan to found a monastic house in Kilbixy. He chose Augustinian canons regular to be its community. These were priests (hence 'canons') who took vows to follow monastic rules (hence 'regular'). They followed specifically the Rule of St Augustine, a set of regulations for monastic life which were based on the writings of Augustine of Hippo (AD 354–430), one of the intellectual heavyweights of early Christianity. That rule had been adopted in early 12th-century Ireland by monastic communities anxious to participate in the reform movement which had started in the later 11th century. The other major monastic rule of the period, the Rule of St Benedict, was observed in Ireland from the 11th century, but it was not until the Cistercians arrived in the 1140s that its observance was widespread on the island.[12] The Anglo-Normans added new Augustinian and Cistercian foundations after the invasion, but that process was nearly over by the second quarter of the 13th century, its momentum lost even before the mendicants (the friars) arrived and soaked up the available patronage.

Two charters, each of the character of a 'foundation charter', are preserved side-by-side at the start of the Tristernagh register.[13] Confusingly, they do not contain the same information. Also, they are not dated. The second charter 'should be the earlier'[14] because there is nothing in it which is not in the first charter, and it contains a little less information, but the two charters are best regarded as near-contemporary. Together, they give us considerable detail on the very earliest phase of Tristernagh, its community, and its resources.

The inconsistencies between the two charters hide from us the precise foundation date of Tristernagh, but knowledge of the general process of foundation of monastic houses and of the role of charters in that process should mitigate any frustration. One could be forgiven for thinking, based on how the concept of foundation is discussed in the scholarly literature, that there was an actual moment of start-up in the life of a monastic house, and that the charter was the contract which, once signed, signaled that a monastic house had officially been founded. In reality, the process of setting up a monastery was long and drawn-out, and a charter, or indeed several charters (including charters of confirmation), might only be written at a late stage when decisions had been made about the site to be occupied and the resourcing of the monastic community.[15] In some cases building work might have begun already, but in others it might have awaited the production of the charter. In the case of Tristernagh, it is apparent from the 'foundation charters' that a considerable amount of preparatory work on the creation of the priory and on the establishment of its funding model had been done before anything was written down, but that building work had not started by then, at least not in earnest.

A full translation of either 'foundation charter' would take up more space than is available, so a paraphrasing of the content of the first and larger charter[16] is outlined here, along with comments on that content. The charter is written in Geoffrey's voice. It begins with him informing those in the present and the future that he has founded a monastery in the territory of Kilbixy in honour of the Blessed Virgin Mary so that the canons will pray for his soul, the souls of his father, mother and wife, Letitia, and for the souls of his ancestors and heirs. Listed then are the resources which are the subject of the grant, as indicated by its title, *Magna Carta G. de Costentin super fundacione domus de Tristernagh cum terris ecclesiis et libertatibus diversis* ('the great charter of Geoffrey de Costentin on the foundation of the house of Tristernagh and its diverse lands, churches and liberties').

The first listed grant is of the land called Tristernagh where the monastery is located, with four carucates of adjacent land. The charter indicates here that the boundaries of these carucates were already established and agreed, which indicates either that the land was already occupied ('established') or that the priory foundation was preceded by a survey of its immediate hinterland ('agreed').

Granted then are the islands of Lough Iron (*Loghyern*), which are near the priory, and whatever part of the lake is known to belong to Geoffrey. This suggests that he did not possess all of the lake, and therefore that the priory did not possess it either. The next grant is difficult to interpret and impossible to map: it refers to a tract of land between the roadway to the church (the parish church in Kilbixy?) and the castle (of 1192), and between the top of that roadway and the site of the mill, and on past the mill-pond and mill-race as far as the land which he had given previously to Agnes, wife of Thurstan de Sandal, and on again as far as the cross of St Columba and, beyond that again, to the house of the old Irish chaplain. He then granted to the canons the right to improve and enlarge the mill (should that be needed) and he guaranteed that the water would not be diverted from the pond and the race. In Conmaicne he granted two carucates beside Lough Iron and between the river Inny and another river, possibly Black river, and one mill and two weirs called Dufcar and Carnegyll. This grant probably relates to the townland of Corry.[17] The weirs might have been on the Inny (a weir is marked on the 1st edition OS map of 1837), and the mill might have been on the Black river (a corn mill is marked on the same map). Geoffrey then permitted the canons to bring the water of the 'Moylle'[18] to the priory through his land via a canal.[19]

The charter then lists some properties outside the Kilbixy area. The canons were granted a toft in the green of Balrothery, Co. Dublin, and the land which had belonged to Radulph the carpenter.[20] They were also granted a messuage (a house and its plot) in Dublin near what is now College Green. Geoffrey granted the canons 10 carucates of the land which he had been granted in Connacht, and the charter's phrasing suggests that he left it up to them to choose where within his Connacht lands they wanted those carucates.

The charter then lists the churches and appurtenances granted to the canons: Kilbixy, Balrothery, 'Tyrclogher' (Clough, Co. Longford?), Rathowen, and Glen, Crossea and Killoe (Co. Longford).

There follows a list of half-carucates which had been owned by Awardus de Moston, Prior Henry of Tristernagh, Robert Moyson, and Agnes de Sandal. These, along with all the land between the bridge in the valley near the cross of St Columba and the priory at Tristernagh, were granted in the charter to the priory, but in exchange for lands which those named owners, and Alured Vigil (Alured the watchman?), were allowed to choose.

Geoffrey then granted five carucates of his wood at 'Kylkareth' (the placename preserves the word *coill*, wood) along with five carucates of adjacent woodland. He granted them also the commonage, the animals of the wood, and the right of pannage (the right to feed pigs in the wood).

A number of grants in the charter were confirmations by Geoffrey of grants and transactions which, it seems, had already been made in the priory's favour. The first, reported somewhat cryptically, is a grant to the canons of a carucate in Kilbixy which had belonged to Robert de Stockbord and which Robert, it seems, had already swopped. Here, and in the other cases, it is not clear if Kilbixy refers to the immediate vicinity of the settlement or to land further out in Moygoish. Next, the grant to the priory by Taurinus the carpenter of lands in Kilbixy, made by charter, was confirmed. Similarly, Geoffrey then confirmed the grant of half a carucate in Kilbixy from Ralph Trivers, and the grant of a mill, its pond and appurtenances by Fulk Fleming. Next, he confirmed the grant of Stephen the archer of a toft in Balrothery, of which Robert of Baldongan held part at a rent of twelve *denarii*; a *denarius* (a unit of currency used in France and Italy) was equivalent to 1d., so twelve was equivalent to a shilling, the normal burgage rent. Next, Geoffrey confirmed the grant of the toft in the settlement (the 'vill') which had previously belonged to Eadric the weaver. Finally, in this list, he confirmed the priory's possession of the land which Felicia, sister of Ornus the cook, had sold to it.

Geoffrey granted to the canons the right to exact tolls from everything sold on their lands. He followed this with a provision which is very unusual in a charter of its type: he allowed them to have a free election of their prior, but then, within a sentence, he carefully withdrew from them the absolute freedom to determine their own affairs.

The charter finishes with a restatement of the guarantee that the priory shall have in perpetuity all that is its due, including tithes, freedom from taxes, and so on, followed by a list of witnesses in this order: Simon de Rochfort (as bishop of Meath), Ralph Petit (as archdeacon of Meath), Patrick Russell *clerico* (parson of Balrothery),[21] Thomas Russell, William Russell, Henry de Rupe *clerico* (parson of Rathaspock),[22] William d'Arcy, Thurstan de Sandal, Alan Gardiner, Richard Russell, Lambert de Londeby, Robert de Northwell (or Burnel), and Hugh the chaplain, author of the charter.

THE DATE OF TRISTERNAGH'S FOUNDATION

Three conclusions about the date of the priory's foundation can be drawn from the two 'foundation charters' and from other charters in the register. Together, they indicate that, despite the evidence for advance planning in the 1190s, the priory was not formally founded before 1200, contradicting Walter Harris's 18th-century view that it was 'much earlier' than 1200.[23]

First, Simon de Rochfort was the bishop of Meath when he licensed the building of the priory church.[24] He had moved the diocesan centre from Clonard to Newtown Trim in 1202 after the former had been attacked two years earlier. From that time on he signed himself the bishop of Meath, not of Clonard,[25] and that was his designation when witnessing the Tristernagh charters. Therefore, work on Tristernagh church was started no earlier than 1202 and no later than 1224, the date of Simon's death. Construction work on monastic sites often began with the laying-out of the cloister, as its metrology was normally continued into the metrology of the other buildings, but the church was the first actual building on any monastic site. A *terminus post quem* of 1202 for the church does not entirely rule out, therefore, the possibility that the priory itself was founded formally before 1200, but it is very unlikely that it had been in existence for a couple of years or more before work on the church started. The *terminus ante quem* of 1224 is less useful to the historian because a date in the 1220s for the foundation is simply too late, especially given that Geoffrey planned the house from well before 1202, but it is useful to the architectural historian who needs fixed dates in order to construct chronologies of forms and features.

Second, the priory had land granted to it in Connacht around the time of its foundation.[26] We know that Connacht cantreds were only added to Geoffrey's portfolio of properties in 1200. The Connacht grants are not spelled out in detail, presumably because Geoffrey did not know those lands himself, and it is unlikely that the priory ever benefitted from them.

Third, Ralph Petit, the first Anglo-Norman archdeacon of Meath who played such a substantial role in the foundation of the priory that he might be regarded as co-founder,[27] is named (as *quondam archidiacono Midie*, former archdeacon of Meath) in three charters issued by Bishop Robert of Ardagh who died in 1224,[28] confirming the *terminus ante quem* of 1224. Petit's prominence in the foundation was a rather unorthodox arrangement in itself, which, combined with the delay in gifting Kilbixy church to a monastery, would tend to indicate that it happened at an early date when the western part of the lordship was most frontier-like. It supports, in other words, a foundation date for Tristernagh in the first decade or so of the 13th century. Petit's close connection with the de Lacys[29] is a reminder that, whatever role the Lord John had played in settling the de Costentins in Meath, it was de Lacy territory. The men with whom Geoffrey had closest contacts, like Petit and de Rochfort, were of the de Lacy circle, and, as I will suggest below, Tristernagh was probably settled with canons from a monastery founded by Hugh de Lacy.

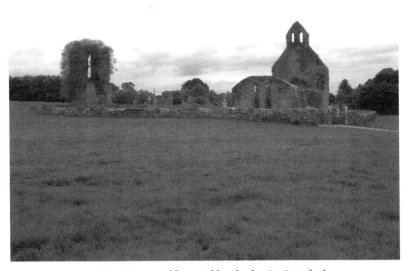

10. The Cistercian abbey at Abbeyshrule, Co. Longford.

The historical evidence indicates, therefore, that Tristernagh Priory was founded early in the first quarter of the 13th century, much closer to 1200 than to 1225. We can buttress this interpretation of its chronology by looking at its architecture on the one hand, and at the pattern of monastic foundation elsewhere in the region on the other. The architectural evidence is discussed below (pp 48–63), but suffice it to say here that it supports a start-date shortly before 1210, with building work continuing as late as the 1220s. The building of two new Cistercian abbeys in the region might also be of relevance in determining Tristernagh's date. The O'Farrells founded a Cistercian abbey at Abbeyshrule (fig. 10) with monks from Mellifont Abbey, Co. Louth, around 1200 while Richard de Tuit had monks from St Mary's in Dublin colonize a new abbey in Abbeylara (fig. 11) sometime before 1210.[30] If he had not already started the process of founding Tristernagh when these (and especially the Anglo-Norman house of Abbeylara) were being founded, Geoffrey would surely have moved quickly to put his own stamp on the monastic landscape.

THE SITE OF THE PRIORY

At the heart of Geoffrey's land-grant was the main church of Uí Moccu Uais, so it was the obvious focus for his new secular settlement. There was another important ecclesiastical site in the vicinity, Templecross, and it determined the

11. The Cistercian abbey at Abbeylara, Co. Longford.

location of the new priory. The present church there is late medieval in date, with a tower above a vault at its west end (fig. 12). In the early 14th century this church, or a predecessor on the site, was a chapel attached to the parish church of Kilbixy,[31] and that relationship was probably a continuation of the arrangement in previous centuries. It was never a parochial church, in other words.

Templecross stands within a small circular graveyard which appears itself to have been off-centre within at least one larger concentric enclosure. These enclosures indicate a site of some antiquity, and certainly older than

12. Templecross Church from the south.

the 12th-century date suggested by the placename element 'Temple'.[32] If Templecross had been a monastic site at one stage, it was no longer functioning as one by the time of the invasion, but a folk memory of monastic observance, even if there had never been such a thing there, might have persuaded Geoffrey to put his own new monastery right beside it.

Another possible lure was the church's status as a place of considerable sanctity in the local landscape. It is not inconceivable that the cross of St Columba, mentioned in the 'foundation charters', was here; there was an ancient cross in the graveyard according to the 1st edition OS map of 1837. Templecross certainly possessed an ancient bell for which a reliquary, the so-called Corp Naomh, was made in the 10th or 11th century.[33] That reliquary survived in tatters into the late middle ages when it was reassembled and repairs were made to it.[34] Assuming the bell and shrine to have been local, the date of the reliquary would support the thesis that Templecross had a stone church when the Anglo-Normans reached the area, and the preservation of the bell within a shrine would suggest that there was pilgrim traffic to the site. Tristernagh was not as remote as it now seems.

The modern visitor to Tristernagh can really only approach it from Templecross (see fig. 2); there is no other demarcated accessway. Templecross itself is accessible by two routes leading off a main road, and one of them – the older, because it approaches from the west? – is recorded on the 1st edition

OS map as *Bohereennamarve*, the small road of the dead.[35] Its line continued past
Templecross in a straight direction towards the priory, and this latter stretch
can be identified as the 'single straight road for entrance' which was recorded in
1540.[36] There was a small bridge over a stream at the end of the road; the small
fragments that survive seem to be medieval. It is reasonable to conclude that
Geoffrey extended the roadway that led to Templecross, converting its ancient
chapel into a gateway chapel for his new priory.

WHY AUGUSTINIAN CANONS REGULAR?

The perception of the Anglo-Norman conquest and colonization of Ireland as
a predominantly military affair does an injustice to the role of Anglo-Norman
churchmen in effecting profound change in late 12th- and 13th-century Ireland.
Authority was claimed over existing ecclesiastical institutions, Englishmen were
appointed to senior ecclesiastical offices, and English monks and canons were
given opportunities to settle in, and maybe even aspire to lead, new monastic
houses.

On the whole, the transformation of the institution of the church in Ireland
under Anglo-Norman hegemony was not violent, one famous crisis in the
Cistercian order notwithstanding,[37] suggesting that holy orders or monastic
vows had a protective value that transcended political and ethnic divisions. Still,
Anglo-Norman clerics in exposed areas must have been alert to dangers, and
more so in some areas than in others. An attack on Clonard in 1200 forced its
Anglo-Norman bishop, Simon de Rochfort, to seek a relocation of the diocesan
centre to Newtown Trim.[38] Only 5km south of Clonard, the priory of the Holy
Trinity in Ballyboggan, founded around 1200[39] for a community of Anglo-
Norman Augustinian canons regular, had a long cruciform church of almost
military austerity, and one senses from this architecture that its canons, located
near the edge of the bogland, were a little jittery (figs 13, 14).[40] However, in
the Kilbixy area, about 20km to the north-west of Ballyboggan and similarly
located in a frontier area, no such nervousness is apparent in the architecture
of Tristernagh Priory, as will be shown. Geoffrey de Costentin's neighbour to
the north, Richard de Tuit, welcomed Cistercians onto his land at Abbeylara,
and they too were able to build the sort of church which they wanted, without
any concession to the need to protect themselves in a crisis. The north-west
corner of the lordship, despite its proximity to Breifne, must have seemed less
dangerous than parts of its southern boundary.

Why did Geoffrey choose to support a house of Augustinian canons regular
rather than one of Cistercian monks? After all, the site chosen for Tristernagh
Priory was precisely the sort of site favoured by Cistercians: it was distant
from the nearest settlement and it had uncontested agricultural resources on
its doorstep. Of course, Geoffrey might never have considered bringing in

13. Ballyboggan Priory church from the north; the gap on the right marks the site of the demolished north transept.

14. The west end of Ballyboggan Priory church. Note the height of the windows in the side wall.

Cistercians. The order already had native-Irish houses in the general district, at Kilbeggan and Abbeyshrule, the latter founded around the time Geoffrey moved to Meath, while Anglo-Norman Cistercians settled in Abbeylara in the first decade of the 13th century. The dates of Abbeylara and Tristernagh relative to each other are not known, but if the plans for the former were put in place first, Cistercian monks would probably not have been an option for the latter.

We can answer the question 'why Augustinian canons regular at Tristernagh?' in three ways. First, canons and monks did not do the same things; they did not offer the same services. The essence of the difference between them, as famously recorded in a 12th-century treatise, *Libellus de diversis ordinibus et professionibus qui sunt in aecclesia*,[41] was their relationship with solitude at one end of the spectrum and the secular world at the other. Monks were between the hermits and canons on this spectrum, but they were closer to the former than the latter; they balanced contemplation and manual labour, but they generally stayed away from pastoral duties, including employing secular priests to officiate in churches to which they were granted advowson. The author of the *Libellus* described the Cistercians as monks 'who remove themselves far from men'.[42] Canons were much more fully embedded in the world outside the cloister. This had been their tradition for centuries, and one of the motivations behind the reimagining of canonical life during the Gregorian reform of the 11th century was to ensure that they stayed true to the apostolic mission, given the ease with which they had been able to divert from it.[43] The Rule of St Augustine, their manifesto for regular life from the time of the Gregorian reform, was flexible, so the new communities of Augustinian canons regular formed a heterogeneous group. The author of the *Libellus* recognized this. He distinguished between those Augustinian congregations which, 'like the apostles in the world', understood that their mission was to 'teach the people, take tithes, collect offerings in church, remonstrate with delinquents (and) reconcile the corrected and penitent to the church',[44] and those of a more austere and contemplative disposition, such as the Premonstratensians, the Victorines and the Arroasians. Communities answering to all these descriptions were present in Anglo-Norman Ireland, especially the Arroasians.[45] Geoffrey did not intend the community at Tristernagh to fulfill a pastoral role in the Kilbixy area.[46] Of the three more 'austere' Augustinian congregations suited to that non-pastoral role, the Arroasians are the most likely to have been invited to settle at Tristernagh.

Second, choosing between Augustinians and Cistercians was not a simple matter. The new Anglo-Norman Cistercian abbeys in Ireland were first- or second-generation colonies of abbeys in England and Wales, ensuring that their communities were wholly colonial, so founding a new Cistercian house required, then, a commitment from an existing Cistercian house to provide the requisite number of monks of the right ethnic-cultural type. There was no flexibility. Unlike the Cistercians, the Augustinians were not a coherent group, united under an over-arching system of administration. Prior to 1215, when a mandate of the Fourth Lateran Council instructed all religious congregations to institute General Chapters at which the heads of monasteries could convene every few years, the Augustinians did not even constitute a monastic order.[47] So, in the absence of some centralized oversight, there was no barrier to individual Anglo-Norman Augustinian houses in late 12th- and early 13th-century Ireland having, among their brethren, native-born clerics who had been trained in the Rule in the pre-invasion era. Setting up an Augustinian priory was, in that sense, an easier process. Indeed, it was asserted in a charter of the priory of Kells in Ossory that there were no Anglo-Norman canons in Ireland until 1183.[48] Maybe so, but it would be wrong to assume from this that the colonial foundations *only* had such canons *after* 1183. On the contrary, there were probably many of them, and their presence may have helped to protect colonial monasteries against acts of aggression by the native Irish. It is safe to assume that Tristernagh's first cohort of canons had transferred mainly from some other Anglo-Norman Augustinian house, but not that they were all of English or Welsh birth.[49]

The question of where that cohort had been before it settled in Tristernagh brings me to the third answer to the question posed above. In the early 13th century, Geoffrey de Costentin was possibly given the ideal opportunity to embark in earnest on the foundation of his planned monastery. By the turn of the century there were two separate Augustinian houses in Clonard, south-east of Kilbixy. St Peter's Abbey was a native Arroasian foundation of pre-invasion date. St John's Priory was founded by Hugh de Lacy in the 1180s. It served as the cathedral, and its community served as the chapter, for Meath after Simon de Rochfort became bishop in 1192.[50] In the early 13th century, the two foundations were amalgamated (as the Abbey of SS Peter and John), and this is most likely to have been done around the time – 1202 – that Simon moved the diocesan centre from Clonard to Newtown Trim. Gwynn and Hadcock suggested that 'most, if not all, of the Anglo-Norman canons' transferred to Newtown Trim with Simon,[51] implying that the native canons stayed in Clonard. However, Newtown Trim's community was largely if not exclusively colonized from St Thomas's Abbey in Dublin, a Victorine house. Simon's cathedral priory was therefore Victorine too. The Clonard canons would not have been trained in the exacting manners of that particularly scholastic congregation so they could not have gone there. If there was an exodus of canons from Clonard around 1202, as Gwynn and Hadcock thought likely, we should probably identify them as the (Arroasian?) canons who settled in Ballyboggan and Tristernagh.

THE PRIORY ENRICHED

The review of the 'foundation charter' above gives a good impression of the priory's rights and possessions at the time of its foundation. Mapping its lands and agricultural resources as recorded in the totality of charters in the register shows that most of its resources were local to it, but with some outlying possessions within the wider area (fig. 15). Those resources were of several types. Churches and their tithes (see fig. 9) were the priory's principal source of income. Tithes paid to a parish church customarily represented one-tenth of the value of the agricultural produce. It was not an insignificant burden on landholders, but it was, conversely, a valuable revenue stream for the ecclesiastical sector. The practice among lords of gifting to monasteries the tithe revenue issuing to parish churches meant that monastic houses like Tristernagh competed with the likes of St Thomas's Abbey and St Mary's Abbey in Dublin for what was a basic and necessary resource. Tristernagh had tithes from its local churches guaranteed at the outset, as well as from the five fees in Conmaicne,[52] while other churches and their tithes were later gifted to it by other landholders, many of them members of prominent Anglo-Norman families.

The charter evidence provides few hints that any of the arrangements made in respect of parish churches and their tithes were complex. However, records pertaining to Balrothery, preserved elsewhere rather than in the register, show how complex the arrangements could be. Balrothery was a rich parish. It was also a subdivision of Lusk, so the Tristernagh community had to pay Lusk 40s. per annum in compensation for the church, as well as 100s. for a 'fit priest' to serve there. The priory's profit margin was reduced further in the 1220s when it had to pay Lusk £10 (200s.) per annum.[53]

Alongside the churches and tithes were more conventional economic resources. Geoffrey de Costentin granted the priory carucates and half-carucates of land right at the outset, and with that land was the freedom to use it as the canons desired. Other landowners added to the priory's portfolio, but in some cases the land was purchased from them.[54] In most instances the grants merely indicate land, without specifying the quantity in acres or carucates, but in some the amount of land was specified, and it varied from between 10 and 18 acres[55] and many hundreds of acres corresponding to the sizes of fees.[56] Woodland was also granted, including a large expanse in Kilbixy itself. The value of woodland was not confined to building materials and fuel: it was feeding land for animals, especially pigs.[57] In his grant to the priory Geoffrey gave the canons the resources of Lough Iron, insofar as they were his to give (the east side of the island appears not to have been part of his seigniory), and they included two small islands close to the site of the priory. More valuable to the priory was access to running water and the right to own and manage mills. Rights to fish are indicated by grants of fishponds and fishpools; the distinction is unclear but the former might have been artificially created whereas the latter were natural pools in rivers. The grant of the fishery of *Karodothan* to the priory reveals that de Costentin was not entirely altruistic in his grants: the canons owed him 500 eels from the fishery as their annual rent.[58]

It is very unlikely that the priory's portfolio of possessions enlarged after the fourteenth century, so we can regard the register as the full record. Indeed, the

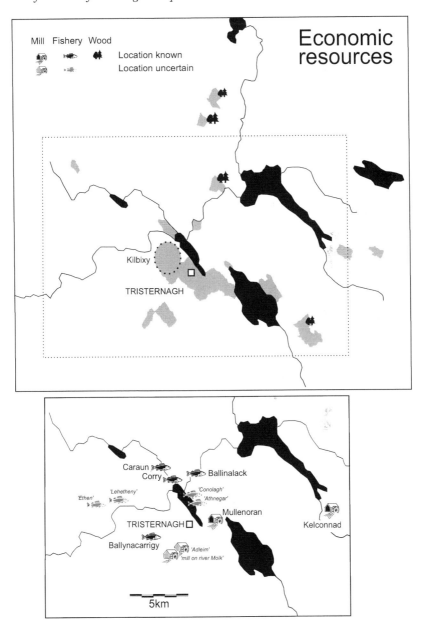

15. The economic resources of Tristernagh Priory. Townlands identified in the register are shaded and the boundaries between them are not shown. Note 1: the spatial extent of Kilbixy itself is uncertain. Note 2: some lands named in the register cannot be identified.

community's ability to draw income from its most distant possessions is likely to
have reduced in the late middle ages. By the early 15th century its buildings had
deteriorated – a good sign of a reduction in real income – and the solution in
1412 was an offer of indulgences, sanctioned in Rome:

> Relaxation, during ten years, of seven years and seven quarantines of
> enjoined penance to penitents, who on the … feasts [of Christmas,
> Circumcision, Epiphany, Easter, Ascension and Corpus Christi,
> Whitsuntide, the Nativity, Annunciation, Purification and Assumption
> of St. Mary the Virgin, the Nativity of St. John Baptist], as far as and
> including [the feast of] SS. Peter and Paul, and that of the dedication, and
> on All Saints, and during the usual octaves and days; and of a hundred days
> to those who, during the said octaves and days, visit and give alms for the
> repair, conservation, or fabric of the Augustinian church and monastery
> of St. Mary, Tristernagh, in the diocese of Meath.[59]

The offer came hard on the heels of controversy within the Tristernagh
community. Three years earlier the archdeacon of Kells was mandated by the
pope to investigate a dispute between the prior, Richard Rowe, the petitioner,
and Richard Hill, one of the canons.[60] It appears that Hill had 'despoiled'
Rowe of the priorship, and that Rowe had produced (the 'cause') papers from
an ecclesiastical court[61] to show that the priorship was rightfully his, but that
the auditor to whom he entrusted the appropriate muniments ('which Rowe
intended to use') had misplaced them. The archdeacon was mandated to
summon Hill 'and others concerned', and 'to decide the cause' (to establish, in
other words, what the earlier ecclesiastical court had ruled). The immediate
outcome of the dispute is not recorded, but by 1412, the year of the offer
of indulgences, Richard Rowe was dead and Richard Hill, 'canon of the
independent Augustinian priory of St Mary, Tristernagh', was provided with
the priory, albeit with up to 30 marks of its value deducted to repay its burdens,
by the anti-pope John XXIII.[62] The case between the two men provides a small
insight into the reality of life and relations behind the priory wall: a common
vocation did not stop canons falling out with each other and engaging in
occasional skullduggery against each other.

CONCLUSION

The evidence of the register provides very valuable data on the foundation and
resourcing of Tristernagh Priory in the early 13th century. Not every question
one might have about the priory and its early history is answered in that source,
but knowledge of the context of its foundation and of the interactions between
the people whose names appear in its charters allows many gaps to be filled.

Informed speculation can fill some of the other gaps. We can claim to know with near certainty the priory's date of foundation, and to know with some confidence why Geoffrey opted for a house of Augustinian canons regular and whence they probably came. We can also identify the priory's economic hinterland as local, maybe regional, but certainly not national. Unlike the two big monastic houses in Dublin (the Augustinian priory, later abbey, of St Thomas the Martyr and the Cistercian St Mary's Abbey), which had possessions in almost every corner of Ireland, the tentacles of Tristernagh's economy did not extend beyond the distance travelled in a few hours on horseback. Balrothery was its only significant distant possession. It is telling that the prior of Tristernagh could be trusted in 1318 to provide independent adjudication in a dispute (over the body of Rohesia de Verdon) between the Dominicans of Trim and the Franciscans of Mullingar;[63] Tristernagh's world was so self-contained geographically that neither mendicant community was considered a neighbour, so neither was advantaged by having the judgement come from the monastery on the other side of Lough Iron.

The absence of a functioning centralized authority – a general chapter – ensured that Augustinian houses like Tristernagh were fundamentally local institutions. In at least one sense, however, Tristernagh was not local. Its architecture spoke of a geographical entity much larger than western Meath: the world of Gothic. It spoke more eloquently of that world than most rural Augustinian priories of the early 13th century in Ireland.

3. A colonial architecture: Gothic Tristernagh

Angelo Mario Bigari and Gabriel Beranger visited Tristernagh in late summer 1779, almost two-and-half centuries after it had been dissolved, and set about making a record of its church, which was all that survived the post-dissolution period. Peter Harbison has valuably documented the circumstances of their partnership.[1] Artists of exceptional ability, they had been brought together by William Burton Conyngham and the short-lived Hibernian Antiquarian Society to record using illustrations the ancient and historic monuments in Ireland. They toured Connacht as a pair in 1779, travelling with an itinerary and letters of introduction to landed gentry provided by Conyngham. At the end of the tour they returned to Dublin via Tristernagh and Multyfarnham. Their visit to Tristernagh was on 16 August, and was in the company of Captain Murray at whose house, Mount Murray on Lough Owel, they had spent the previous night.[2] Murray might have been invited along to make sure they could get access to Tristernagh: the landlord who owned the property was Sir Pigott William Piers[3] and it seems that he was not especially well-disposed to the antiquarian project.

The church which faced them as they headed into the estate from Templecross had not changed much physically since the early 13th century. The priory had continued to function through the middle ages, as we have seen, but apart from the insertion of a tower into the western two bays of the nave (fig. 16), possibly in response to mid-15th-century insecurities,[4] it looked much as it had done in Geoffrey de Costentin's time. The long drive towards it from Templecross gave them ample time to absorb what was a special building.

A 'WANTON OUTRAGE'

Sir Pigott William's family had owned the site since 1562. Captain William Piers (c.1510–1602), originally from Piers Hall near Ingleton in Yorkshire, had spent most of his career engaged in military, political and commercial pursuits in Ulster.[5] He received a number of Irish properties in 1562, including Tristernagh, and he chose to retire to the priory in 1582. His son, Henry, succeeded to the title and converted to Catholicism. He married the daughter of the archbishop of Dublin, Dr Thomas Jones. He died in 1623 and was buried in Templecross where he had erected 'a vault and monument' in 1620. His son, Sir William Piers, born 1598, married Martha, the eldest daughter of Sir James Ware.[6] He

16. The tower in the west end of the nave of Tristernagh, viewed from the east; note the corbelled parapet.

died in 1638. His son, Henry, born 1628, had the title of 1st Baronet from 1660. Following in the footsteps of his maternal grandfather, Sir James Ware, Sir Henry developed an interest in antiquarianism, and wrote his *Chorographical description of the county of Westmeath* in 1682; it was not published until almost a century later. He may have instilled in his immediate successors (including the hapless 3rd Baronet, killed by an overdose of opium in 1734)[7] a respect for the old ruin that allowed it survive through most of the Georgian period, a period during the later stages of which the estate was apparently struggling.[8] The priory's luck ran out when Sir Pigott William succeeded to the baronetcy in 1746/47.

In 1783, in an act described by James Norris Brewer as one of 'wanton outrage', the baronet demolished the church.[9] Yet it was not necessarily an act of casual or vindictive vandalism. Intending to extend his house into the space that it occupied, or to use its stone for some other building work, the baronet probably saw it not as a heritage monument to be maintained but as a resource to be exploited. His crime, as Brewer might have described it, was that he exploited, or appeared to have exploited, the medieval inheritance differently from his predecessors. By the time he became baronet, the old priory had already been reduced to its church by acts of demolition by one or more of his predecessors. The two-storeyed, mainly brick-built, domestic building on

17. The only 18th-century domestic building at Tristernagh.

the site of the monastic refectory (fig. 17) was probably built by one of those predecessors.[10]

When Bigari and Beranger pulled up outside Tristernagh House on 16 August 1779, their host was possibly already thinking about demolishing the church. If so, he said nothing to them; Beranger's testimony contains no hint that he and his travelling companion knew that the building's days were numbered. Sir Pigott William certainly did not hide his intentions as the actual date of demolition approached, because Lord Sunderlin of nearby Baronstown House, alerted to its impending destruction, offered to purchase the venerable old monument at a good price, solely with a view to its preservation.[11] He was turned down. So too were other neighbours who, Brewer tells us, 'earnestly solicited' the landlord to preserve the ruins.[12] Sunderlin's request was not entirely reasonable: the medieval church was, after all, attached to the Piers family residence.

THE 1779 RECORD

Beranger, Dutch-born of French Huguenot extraction, is the better known of the two artists who arrived at Tristernagh that day, and his work has long been identified as an important source of information for monuments altered or

18. Bigari's drawing of Tristernagh church from the north-west.

destroyed since the end of the 18th century.[13] The Italian-born Bigari, who had probably come to Ireland as a scene-painter, is first recorded working in Dublin's Smock Alley Theatre in 1772.[14] His role on the tour of 1779 was to draw the general views of the monuments while Beranger took responsibility for drawing architectural features and ground plans.[15] The men aimed to record on paper what they saw, but they developed a habit of editing out structures and features which they believed they could identify as later additions and alterations. Beranger reported that they were rather proud of these interventions:

> we are become most terrible levelers. Since in our drawings we level without quarter, all those vile walls, with which ignorance had spoiled the elegance of Antiquity, we restore every thing on its ancient footing, opening arches, doors and windows.[16]

Bigari produced two very good drawings of the priory church at Tristernagh, one looking at its exterior from a vantage point to the north-west (fig. 18) and one looking down the nave towards the east end (fig. 19).[17] Engravings based on these drawings were subsequently published in the second volume of Grose's *Antiquities* in 1791.[18] These engravings are exact copies of the originals, although some of the features were 'sharpened' (an unhelpful 'improvement') and some of the people whom Bigari drew in the foreground of each drawing were removed.

19. Bigari's drawing of Tristernagh church interior from the west.

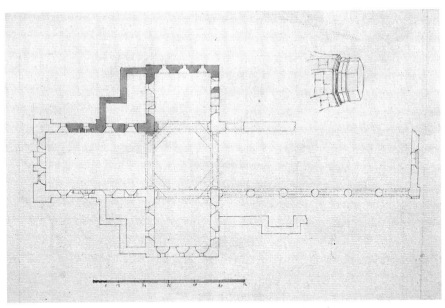

20. Beranger's plan of Tristernagh church.

Beranger also produced a plan of the church (fig. 20).[19] It was not published in *Antiquities*.

Beranger's commentary on Tristernagh is a very valuable gloss on the two drawings and the ground plan:

> Augt 16th. This Abby was magnificent, and formerly larger; part of the entrance compose at present a portion of the dwelling of Sr Pigot Piers Bart and some parts are offices, we restored in the drawg its primitive state as much as possible, opening the arches, which were closed with masonry. it is of good workmanship, of blackish stone, the steeple is uncommon being an octogone on the top of a square and tho multilated, is still 74 feet high; it is supported by a grand arch like those of Boyle and Ballintober which is at present 39 feet high, and was undoubtedly higher as the ground is raised so as to cover the bases of the columns, part of this arch serves for Deary and part a stable, nothing of the windows remain but their apertures, the columns are octogone and their capitals plan. See plan etc. No 54.

We are very fortunate indeed that Bigari made two drawings from slightly different angles. Both drawings show some of the same features, so the general accuracy of each is confirmed by the other, and comparison between the drawings and the small fragment of architecture which survives today offers further confirmation.[20] Similarly, Beranger's plan of the church can be matched with the drawings and its scale can be confirmed by examining the surviving fragments. The record of Tristernagh made by Bigari and Beranger is, then, very good. There is only one obvious mistake. The arches of the nave arcade were not round, as Bigari drew them in his 'second view' (fig. 19), but pointed. They were possibly blocked at the time, so he had to guess their shapes. Still, from the point of view of the architectural historian it is a bad mistake because, were it not for the surviving fabric, one would date incorrectly an important feature of the priory. Identifying this mistake naturally raises questions about other features in the drawings, and these are taken into account in the analysis which follows. Problems aside, we must be grateful that the two men, probably fatigued at the end of their tour and with their homes in Dublin beckoning, made a concerted effort to capture with some accuracy the old priory. A number of the monuments which they visited on their tour have also been lost in the intervening years, but from the perspective of architectural history none was as important as Tristernagh, and no loss can be as lamented.

TRISTERNAGH'S CLAUSTRAL PLAN

As an English priory of Augustinian canons regular, Tristernagh was quite conventional in its overall layout. It had a claustral plan from the time of its foundation.[21] The design principle of this type of plan originated in monastic architecture on the Continent a few centuries before the Anglo-Norman invasion of Ireland, and was used everywhere in medieval Europe with relatively little variation, so it is quite easy to reconstruct the basic layout of Tristernagh in its entirety several centuries after its destruction, and even to suggest the specific sizes of its elements (fig. 21).

In brief, the medieval monastic claustral plan takes its name from the *claustrum* or cloister. This was an enclosed courtyard of square or rectangular plan, ringed by covered walkways (or 'alleys' as they are sometime termed), outside which again on three or four sides were the church and the monastic buildings, arranged as a continuous suite. The central court was sometimes used as a small garden area or even as a cemetery, but any practical use to which it was put was always incidental to its main purpose, which was to be the space around which the monastic buildings were placed in ranges. The arrangement of those claustral buildings was consistent.

The church, the most important building, was normally positioned on the north side of the cloister, leaving all the other buildings on its south side. The less frequent alternative position for the church, favoured by medieval mendicant friars in Ireland, for example, was on the south side of the cloister,

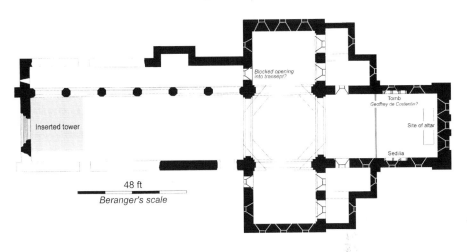

Inserted tower

Blocked opening into transept?

Tomb
Geoffrey de Costentin?

Site of altar

Sedilia

48 ft

Beranger's scale

Tristernagh House

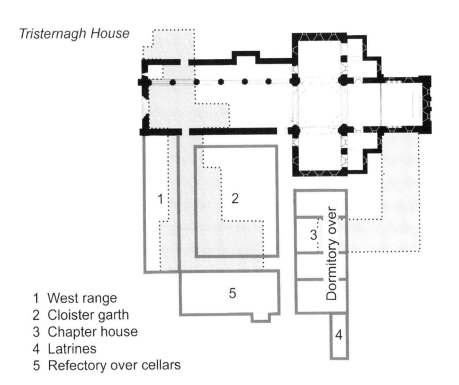

1 Dormitory over

2

3

4

5

1 West range
2 Cloister garth
3 Chapter house
4 Latrines
5 Refectory over cellars

21. Reconstruction of the plan of Tristernagh Priory.

in which case the entire monastic plan was simply flipped over, leaving the claustral buildings in the same arrangement but on the north side. Directly across the cloister opposite the church was the refectory, the dining hall. Its position was determined by the position of the church: if the church was on the north side of the cloister the refectory was on the south side, and *vice versa*. The refectory could be a single-storeyed building with a high roof, or it could be a two-storeyed building with the eating space above a basement or cellar. The refectory building could take up an entire range but sometimes there were flanking service buildings, one of them being the kitchen. Regardless of the position of the church relative to the cloister, the eastern claustral range was the location of the chapter house or chapter room, a ground-level space so-named because a chapter of the monastic rule was read there every day. This room was fairly central in the range, and was flanked by other rooms, the functions of which varied. One of the rooms was usually a parlour, a room in which members of a community were allowed time-limited conversation. The upper storey of the east range was the dormitory or dorter, the sleeping area. At one end of it was the church, visited by members of the monastic community in the middle of the night during the cycle of prayer known as the Divine Office, and at the other end was the toilet block, also known as the reredorter or necessarium. The western claustral range did not have prescribed functions, which gave monasteries flexibility. Occasionally there was no west range: for example, Bridgetown Priory in Co. Cork, also Augustinian and only a little younger in date than Tristernagh, had a wall on the west side of its cloister.[22] But a west range was useful for storage and for services associated with the refectory. It was also a good place in which to put a parlour, a room where conversation was permitted, sometimes even with visiting family members. The Cistercians used west ranges to accommodate *conversii*, the lay brethren within their communities.

So, the basic shape of Tristernagh Priory is fairly easy to reconstruct. It is also possible, despite the priory's near-total destruction, to reconstruct the plan as it was deployed specifically at Tristernagh. There are two keys to working out the details of the priory's claustral plan. The first is the church, the architecture of which is discussed below. The second is the representation of Tristernagh House on the 1st edition OS map of 1837. We know that this was the house site before the 1783 demolition because Beranger tells us in 1779 that the Piers residence was attached to the west end of the church. It occupied the site of the west range, and probably incorporated some of that range's medieval architecture. We can also tell from the irregularity of the plan of Tristernagh House on the map that it was a multi-phase structure, from which we can conclude, first, that the development of the house had been somewhat ad hoc, and second, that Sir Pigott William Piers did not fully replace after 1783 the residence which he inherited.

We can detect the ghost of the claustral scheme if we scale up (and rotate about 10° for planimetric accuracy) the plan of the Piers residence as it is shown on the 1st edition map. The east-west width of the cloister can be worked out from the plan of the church and the position of Tristernagh House. This means that, allowing for the customary slype or passage on its east side, we can also determine the length of the refectory. The cloister's length was apparently greater, allowing one to reconstruct a slype and several rooms at ground-floor level.

The basic architecture of the chapter house and refectory is not difficult to reconstruct. Comparison with other priories would suggest that the former was originally no wider than the east range itself, that stone benches ran along its north and south walls, and that its east wall was lit by three windows. The refectory can be reconstructed as a two-storeyed structure, which was the norm in Augustinian monasteries. The upstairs room was the actual dining space, and it is understood that this was because the Last Supper was held in an upper room.[23] Comparative evidence suggests that access was by internal stairs at the west end of the building and that the pulpitum from which a member of the community read aloud from a sacred text during meal time was contained within a projection at the opposite end of the building. Washing hands before meals was an important ritual and comparative evidence would again suggest that the laver – the basin supplied with water from containers or perhaps fed with rain water by lead pipes – was set into the outside wall of the refectory near the external point of entry.

THE PRIORY CHURCH

Angelo Mario Bigari drew Tristernagh Church as a free-standing building, giving the impression that the claustral complex was lost by then. His panoramic view from a patch of empty ground on its north-west side shows further empty ground behind it on the south side where the cloister would have been. Looking through the west doorway one can see a figure of a man crossing in the direction of a group of people dancing around an individual who is holding a pole with something tied to it.[24] When the two artists visited the priory in 1779 there was no such view through the west doorway; it had been blocked by the tower mentioned above. Nor was there a view of the place where Bigari put the dancing figures. Here, the Piers residence was in the way. Beranger noted that 'part of the entrance [to the church] compose at present a portion of the dwelling of Sr [William] Pigot Piers Bart', and that can be confirmed at the site today (fig. 22).

Much of the medieval façade survived that same landlord's demolition of the church, but the fabric on that façade's south (or right-hand) side is from that

22. Entrance façade of Tristernagh church; note the remains of one of three windows in the wall above the doorway, and of an original 13th-century window in the low (aisle) wall on the left.

18th-century dwelling, if not from an early 19th-century rebuilding. That later fabric includes a pilaster (or buttress) which was built to imitate the surviving medieval pilaster on the north (or left-hand) side. The imitation pilaster was not built in the right position relative to the church doorway, which is why that doorway now appears off-centre. Brick window-surrounds were built into this imitation, presumably to balance other windows in the now-demolished house, but they must have been blind windows because there is medieval fabric directly behind them. The design of the brick-surrounds suggests that they could date from well into the 19th century.

As noted above, Beranger admitted that on their tour he and Bigari exercised artistic license, leaving out of their drawings any features which they judged not to be original. Thus, in the case of Tristernagh, the Piers residence was not shown. The tower inserted into the west end of the nave was also left out. So too was the 'Deary [dairy] and part a stable' installed under one of the crossing arches.[25] Even if no admission had been made about their editorial policy in respect of later features, one could determine easily that Bigari had stripped away certain things. Most obviously, the ruin is depicted as very 'clean': there is a garnish of ivy on the west gable and some stones are shown scattered around the place in both drawings, but there are no indications of burials on the inside. The interval between the priory's dissolution and its acquisition by the Piers family was too short for many post-medieval burials to accumulate under the church floor, but there would have been medieval burials there, especially at its east end. Bigari would have seen the evidence of this, but he did not include it.

Had the church been free-standing and as well-manicured as it is depicted, Bigari would probably have drawn it from another angle, instead of choosing two angles close together. Other structures, including but not confined to the Piers residence, must have prevented him getting a clear view of the church from a suitable vantage point to the south or the east. In his view of the interior one can see a pair of post-medieval chimneys rising over the east gable and they must have belonged to some substantial later structure blocking a good view of the church from the east.

One original medieval wall was left out of Bigari's panoramic view: this is the short, half-gabled, medieval wall on the north (left-hand) side of the façade (compare figs 18 and 22). This was omitted not because it was regarded as one of those 'vile walls, with which ignorance had spoiled the elegance of antiquity' but because it blocked part of the view of the arcade, a feature he wanted to show in its full glory. As noted, it is entirely possible that the entire arcade had been blocked by the late 18th century and that he did not see that the original arches were pointed. Blocking might also have disguised the surviving clerestory windows – one remains to this day – above the arcade. Other medieval features might also have been observed but not depicted. Do the omissions affect our trust in these drawings as a record of an important medieval building? The answer is a qualified 'no'; features omitted are much less problematic for the researcher than features invented.

Beranger's plan and Bigari's two views are perfectly synchronized, and that is critical to the study of the building. There is nothing in the two views that one cannot identify in the plan, which builds trust in Beranger's survey of features in parts of the building which Bigari did not draw. Their work shows that the church had, from the outset, a more sophisticated plan than all but a very small number of other medieval Augustinian churches in Ireland. Were it still standing it would be lauded as one of the most important medieval buildings in Ireland, and for that reason it merits the space given here to a description and an analysis.

The choir and presbytery
The church was transeptal in plan. It had a square crossing with square transepts on either side, a moderately long choir and presbytery to the east, and a nave with a single north aisle. It is appropriate to start this discussion with the choir and presbytery at the east end, as this was the part of every church where construction work began.

The eastern limb at Tristernagh – the space east of the crossing – was a rectangle almost twice as long as it was wide. Its external corners had, according to Beranger, clasping buttresses of classic 13th-century type. It would have been divided internally into two parts of unequal length. The eastern part, probably a square in plan, was the presbytery, where the high altar was located. To the west was the choir, where the canons sang the Divine Office from their stalls. There would not have been enough room between the crossing and the presbytery to accommodate the full complement of canons, especially as there were doorways opening from the choir into the adjacent transeptal chapels, so the choir stalls must have continued into the crossing. That would not have been unusual. It must have been the scheme at Newtown Trim as well.[26]

Beranger's plan offers a more convincing representation of the eastern limb of the church than Bigari's drawing, and one must suspect that they did not converse when they were working on that part of the church. Both agree on the number of windows – three in the east wall and four in each of the side walls – and on the doorways into the transeptal chapels, but there the similarities between their drawings end.

Bigari's drawing of arched recesses underneath the windows makes no sense in a medieval context. Although he did show some typically crude post-dissolution blocking of the middle window in the east wall, I think that he did not recognize the full extent of later blocking elsewhere, and that the recesses are probably a case in point: all of the recesses are depicted below windows, which suggests to me that the windows above the recesses were all a little longer originally and that those recesses were the product of later blocking. If this interpretation is correct, they might not have been as near to the floor of the church as Bigari indicates, because the windows at the east ends of monastic churches were, with few exceptions (such as Ballyboggan), normally higher than eye-level. It is important to recall, however, Beranger's statement that 'the ground is raised' (presumably by rubble and burials) inside the church. If we allow that there was a build-up of a metre or more on the floor, the drawing would make more sense.

One possible problem with this interpretation is that it presupposes that the sills of the original windows were all at the same height off floor-level, whereas the custom in medieval ecclesiastical architecture was to elevate the side-windows to allow the space needed for the liturgical architecture that was always located along the side walls. Indeed, Beranger placed on his plan a sedilia – a set of seats for those officiating at Mass – in the south wall, and directly opposite he placed a similar feature which was probably intended to represent a tomb of the type that normally had its mensa used for Easter rituals.[27] He wrote that he and Bigari 'restored in the drawg its primitive state as much as possible, opening the arches, which were closed with masonry', and yet Bigari did not see evidence of such liturgical features. On balance, the likelihood is that in the original early 13th-century design of Tristernagh's east end there were long lancets and one short lancet in each side wall, and that the sills of the longer side-wall lancets were level with those of the end-wall windows lancets. This was also the arrangement at Newtown Trim in the period 1202–16.[28] There is no evidence in the record of 1779 of late medieval alterations to the east limb of the church.

The transepts and transeptal chapels

There are some differences between the work of the two artists on this part of the church as well but they are small and none creates a serious problem of interpretation. Here, Bigari's record is the more convincing in matters of detail, and without special pleading.

Beranger's plan reveals the transepts to have been square in outline, with two chapels off each transept, arranged in a stepped, or échelon, plan. The longer chapels at Tristernagh – those which flanked the choir – had entrances from both the choir and the transepts. The points of entry to the transeptal chapels are shown as round-arched, and one of Bigari's drawings suggests a variety of treatments of those arches: the doors off the choir had plain arches, the doors from the transepts into the chapels nearest the choir had soffit (underside) arches springing from tapering corbels, and the doors into the outer chapels had recessed arches.

Versions of échelon plans are present in the European architectural repertoire from Carolingian times, and the concept was first deployed in Ireland before the Anglo-Norman invasion.[29] The plan of Tristernagh's transepts can be paralleled easily, and in association in some cases with single-aisled naves, in northern English and Scottish Augustinian priory churches, such as Bolton in Yorkshire, Jedburgh in the Scottish Borders (formerly Roxburghshire), both 12th century, and in the earlier 13th-century phase at Lanercost in Cumbria, as well as in Newtown Trim (1202–16).[30] The same plan type was used in St Canice's Cathedral, Kilkenny, and probably also in Ferns Cathedral, Co. Wexford, two 13th-century rebuildings of native cathedrals.[31] Both Bolton and Newtown Trim share with Tristernagh (as well as with the early 13th-century Augustinian priory church of Athassel, Co. Tipperary) doorways from the choir into the transeptal chapels. The dates of all these parallels (fig. 23) are worth noting.

The fenestration drawn by Bigari in the Tristernagh transepts is exceptionally interesting. First, the west wall of each transept had two large windows, and it is probable that each window was aligned with an entry to a chapel in the wall opposite. Second, the end-walls of the two transepts had tripartite fenestration: three tall, round-arched (?) windows of equal height, with two smaller windows, also round-arched (?), higher up in the lower part of the gable, and a quatrefoil at the top of the gable. There are parallels for this arrangement, the most exact in Ireland being in early Cistercian churches: the east end of Duiske Abbey, Graiguenamanagh, Co. Kilkenny, built before 1210, had a similar arrangement, including two round-arched windows and a quatrefoil, while the east end of Dunbrody Abbey, Co. Wexford, probably built by 1216, was similar in design but with graded lancets and a simple window instead of a quatrefoil.[32] Did the transepts at Abbeylara look like this too?

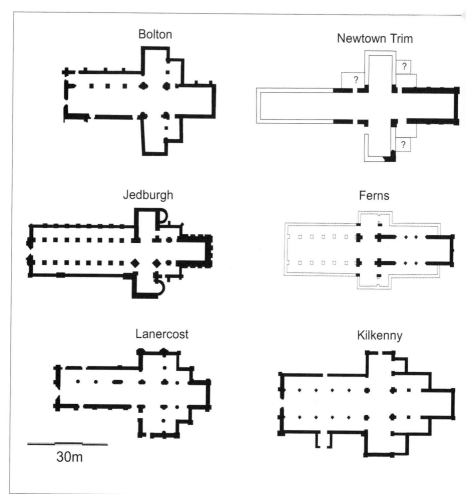

23. Comparative Augustinian church plans.

The crossing

The crossing was square and was famously surmounted by an octagonal tower with a fairly large round-arched window in the centre of each face. In 1682, Sir Henry Piers, who lived beside the church, wrote that it had in its centre 'a tower or steeple, raised on the four innermost corners of the cross, from each of which corners the wall as it rises slopeth off until the whole is brought into an octagon; whence forward the tower riseth about thirty foot in eight sides, in each of which is a window'.[33] The description tallies with the Bigari drawings. Beranger indicated the outline of the octagon on his plan.

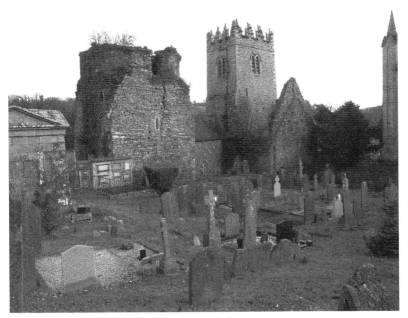

24. Inistioge belfry.

Towers of this shape and in this position are found in north-west Europe, including in England, from the 11th century on. They were used in churches of all types, even (as in England) in mendicant churches. Many were belfries, but some were lanterns, designed to allow light descend into the space below. The Tristernagh tower was probably also a lantern: the Bigari drawing indicates that there was no floor below the octagon. There is no reason to think that it was also a belfry: lantern towers were not bell towers.

Tristernagh's octagon was an original, early 13th-century, feature. Although there is no exact parallel in Ireland for it, there are plenty of parallels for aspects of it. First, of the small number of octagonal and semi-octagonal towers in Ireland, most date from the early 13th century, and they include examples in non-ecclesiastical contexts (as at Trim Castle, Co. Meath, Carlingford Castle, Co. Louth, and the largely destroyed Butter Gate, Drogheda, Co. Louth). There are two good parallels for Tristernagh among Irish belfry towers: St Mary's Church, Askeaton, Co. Limerick, and Inistioge Priory (Augustinian), Co. Kilkenny (fig. 24). Second, crossing arches of the width of those at Tristernagh are characteristic of the early 13th century; there is a contemporary Cistercian example at Abbeylara (see fig. 11), also in the lordship of Meath. The Tristernagh arch cannot be much younger: it was not so much that the fashion for wide crossing arches went into decline in Ireland after a few decades of the

13th century but that the orders of monks (Cistercian) and canons (Augustinian) who built churches requiring such arches lost out in the patronage stakes to the mendicants who arrived in the 1220s and 1230s and did not favour cruciform churches. Third, Bigari drew corbels supporting the soffit (underside) arches, and even though he drew them as V-shaped in the manner of 15th-century corbels, what he must have observed given the size of the arches were tapering corbels of the type that one finds underneath soffit arches in many 12th- and 13th-century monastic churches, especially Cistercian.

The nave
The nave of the church was a long rectangle with a single aisle on the north side. It is appropriate to begin by discussing the points of entry to it.

There were four doorways. Two of them were processional doorways in the south wall and they connected with the cloister. Bigari drew the main processional doorway at the east end of this wall; this was the doorway through which the canons of the priory (having worked in the cloister, met in the chapter house, or eaten in the refectory) entered the church for the Divine Office. It was relatively wide, as befits an opening of such importance in the ritual life of the priory. It seems to have been round-arched, which would point to an early date in the priory's history. Canons who entered the church through this doorway would not have been fully visible from the nave: a screen would have extended across the width of the church, connecting the plain wall on its south side with one of the piers of the nave on the opposite side. A little further to the west in the same south wall of the church was the second doorway off the cloister but it was gone by the late 18th century. The third doorway is that which survives in the west wall (see fig. 22). Its stone surround is so large that one wonders whether it was simply an outer frame with a smaller doorway inside it. If not, there was a very large two-leaf doorway here, and the sight of the interior of the church when it was opened must have been very impressive. Its grandeur suggests that it was not a doorway through which the church was entered casually, but was reserved for special occasions and for any special penitents who visited. The final doorway was at the west end of the north wall of the aisle. This was the normal location for an entrance into a church with a north aisle.

The south wall of the nave was plain apart from a row of windows bringing light in from above the cloister roof. A pair of (round-arched?) windows survived to Bigari's time. On the other side of the church, the arcuated wall separating the main body of the nave from the north aisle had six arches, with clerestory windows directly above the piers. Each arch was two-ordered and pointed with chamfers, and sprang from asymmetrically concave capitals of polygonal shape with strongly rolled imposts and astragals, and carried on polygonal piers or responds. Only two of the arches remain in situ, one very damaged, while there survives in situ just one respond and none of the piers (fig. 25). There is one ex situ fragment of a pier with part of a capital.

25. The remains of the arcade in Tristernagh church.

The surviving pilaster on the façade marks on the outside of the church the position of the arcade on the inside. The practical function of the pilaster was to stabilize externally the façade at the point where the arcuated wall was pushing against it internally, but it also had an aesthetic purpose: pilasters were used to articulate external wall surfaces in Norman and early Angevin-period buildings, even when they were not particularly needed for buttressing. The missing pilaster at Tristernagh, replaced in the late 18th or early 19th century, would have been entirely an aesthetic feature as it had no real structural function. The surviving pilaster is strikingly plain, which would not be inconsistent with a date in the early 13th century, and it projects outwards from the wall more boldly than was normal for such features.

Turning now to the matter of dating, Irish medieval ecclesiastical architecture was very conservative from as early as the second quarter of the 13th century, and nowhere is that conservatism more apparent than in the designs of arcuated walls. The Tristernagh wall can be paralleled in churches built over a period of several centuries, but northern English and Scottish parallels help to secure a date for it in the early 13th century. One parallel is the design of the supports and arches in the nave aisle arcade in the church of the Augustinian priory of Brinkburn in Northumberland (fig. 26). Building work here started in the 1180s,[34] so the nave arcade is probably of the 1190s. A second parallel is a little later: the design of the nave arcade and of the transept and choir aisle arcades

26. The nave of Brinkburn Priory church.

added in the early to mid-13th century to the church of the Augustinian priory
of Lanercost in Cumbria.[35]

If the Tristernagh arcade dates from the 13th century, the aisle must have
been an original feature of the nave. Supporting evidence is both structural and
comparative. Regarding the former, there is a much-damaged 13th-century
window in the aisle's west wall (see fig. 22) which is clearly in its original
setting. One can tell its date from the shape of the arch on the outside but more
especially from the impressions of a timber frame in the mortar on the underside
of the window's internal splay; the technique of building arches using timber
frames rather than wicker mats is characteristic of Anglo-Norman work.[36]

The comparative evidence for dating the aisle to the early 13th century is even more convincing. With only one certain exception, the Augustinian priory churches built in early 12th-century England were cruciform in plan with aisleless naves, but by the end of the century single aisles (always on the north side, because of the position of the cloister) had become more common (see fig. 23 above), and were either added to older churches in phases of redevelopment or were built *ab initio* in new foundations.[37] The new aisles had no liturgical functions, but they offered a new option for circulation within their churches, allowing movement from the west end to the altar that by-passed both the nave and the crossing. Tristernagh's nave plan was, therefore, a classic of its type.

AESTHETIC COLONIZATION: TRISTERNAGH'S STYLISTIC WORLD

Tristernagh church was a fairly remarkable building in and of itself: the spatial provision for liturgy was exceptionally large by the Augustinian standard in Ireland, and no other Augustinian church is known to have had a lantern tower over its crossing. The church is even more remarkable when one considers its context. There was no cathedral chapter attached to it to justify the relative opulence, especially of its east end. And there is nothing in Geoffrey's profile as an Anglo-Norman lord, relatively high though it was, and certainly nothing about the Kilbixy district itself, which would lead one to expect Tristernagh to have had a church of such quality. While we cannot explain *why* Tristernagh church was 'better' than many other churches of its era, we can at least provide a contextual explanation of its architecture.

The suggestion was made earlier that Tristernagh's canons were Arroasian and that they may have settled there from Clonard after that ecclesiastical site lost its status in 1202. That would not necessarily mean that its masons would have come from there too. On the contrary, Clonard cannot have been the source of Tristernagh's architecture, or of the architecture of Ballyboggan, the other site possibly colonized from Clonard after 1202. To understand why Clonard can be rejected so definitively, but also to understand Tristernagh's national importance (even as a demolished monument), we need to consider very briefly the transformation in ecclesiastical architecture in Ireland in the two decades either side of 1200.

In 1174, a fire destroyed the Romanesque choir of Canterbury Cathedral in south-east England. The community there hired a Frenchman, William of Sens, to build a replacement, and he skillfully oversaw the insertion into the Romanesque shell of a new choir in the style of French Gothic. It was the first work of Gothic in England. During the 1170s the style spread in England, quickly losing its 'Frenchness' and developing instead the characteristics of what is now known as Early English Gothic.[38] This is the Gothic style which the

Anglo-Normans introduced to Ireland. If one had to give a style name to the architecture of Tristernagh church, it would be Early English.

That style was not brought to Ireland by the original invaders; the English had not developed it yet in 1169–70. It first appeared in Ireland in the 1190s. The oldest surviving example is at Grey Abbey, Co. Down, a Cistercian house founded in 1193. When St Thomas's Priory in Dublin was given the status of an abbey in 1192, its Romanesque church was very likely rebuilt or at least modernized in the Early English Gothic style, so there is a strong case for considering it the first work of Gothic in Ireland, our equivalent of the Canterbury choir.[39] The two Augustinian houses in Clonard were already in existence in the 1190s, so their architecture cannot have been Gothic. Therefore, Clonard is not Tristernagh's source.

Rather than search for a single source, we might consider Tristernagh one of a group of early Gothic Augustinian churches in Ireland, with St Thomas's at the head of the sequence chronologically. St Thomas's design is not yet known – archaeological excavations might yet reveal it – but there is no reason to think that it was imitated in those Augustinian churches built immediately after it, except perhaps in the cathedral priory of Newtown Trim, laid out around 1202. The oldest surviving non-Cistercian work of Gothic architecture in Ireland, Newtown Trim was a long cruciform church with one chapel (maybe two?) off each transept, a crossing tower and an aisleless nave (see fig. 23). The absence of an aisle on its north side means that Tristernagh, started within a few years of it, was not a slavish copy of it. That indicates that there was more than one pattern book for Gothic architecture, more than one set of ideas about the planning of Augustinian churches, and more than one team of masons, in the lordship of Meath at the very start of the 13th century.

Is Tristernagh, insofar as we can now claim its architecture to be known, albeit in absentia, any more important than Newtown Trim or Ballyboggan in our understanding of the early history of the lordship of Meath? In one sense the answer is 'no'. These three buildings were different from each other in small ways, which gives them equal importance. But in another sense the answer is 'yes'. It is the building which tells us that builders trained in the new Gothic style – we cannot say where they were trained – could criss-cross Meath, venture into slightly dangerous corners and work on quite elaborate commissions, even before any claim could be made that the land was fully secure and the process of subinfeudation complete.

With Newtown Trim Cathedral church and the priory churches of Tristernagh and Ballyboggan one witnesses, perhaps, a form of colonization quite different from that attested to in historical sources. It was an aesthetic colonization. These churches were new additions to institutions with pre-invasion histories, but their size and especially their architectural detailing – their aesthetic character – signalled outwardly their alien status. The native Irish were already familiar with the Romanesque style used by first-generation

Anglo-Norman builders in Ireland, and they were especially familiar from the middle of the 12th century with the version of Romanesque used by the Cistercians. But the priory churches of Newtown Trim and Tristernagh, less so Ballyboggan, *looked* different from native Augustinian churches, and in so doing they represented the new political order as potently as any contemporary castle. The Irish fully understood how architectural style conveyed political messages,[40] so we should not doubt that they understood what new buildings such as Tristernagh said about the new colonial ownership of the most venerable tradition, the Christian tradition.

Conclusion

Sir Pigott William Piers' decision in 1783 to demolish most of what was left of the church of Tristernagh Priory earned him immediate opprobrium and the promise that it would not be forgotten nor be forgiven. Recalling almost 40 years later the failed attempts of his neighbours to persuade him not to dismantle the priory ruins, James Norris Brewer described Piers as a 'tasteless and unfeeling demolisher' and advised that 'the name Tristernagh should never be mentioned without an expression of contempt (as regards this transaction) towards him'.[1] In the early 19th century, Henry Upton, a local politican and antiquarian in Westmeath, recorded a tradition that a disturbance of the graveyard at the 'abbey' – the cemetery that features in one of the priory's 13th-century charters[2] – was responsible for a curse on Sir Pigott William and for the 'misfortunes' and 'disasters' that befell the Piers family and their residence at Tristernagh.[3] If Sir Pigott William has, in the afterlife, been spared some of the contempt that Brewer and others felt was his due, it is because so few people go to see the site and take the opportunity to reflect on what was lost.

Time spent staring at the 1779 drawings as an architectural-historian persuaded me that Tristernagh Priory could have a particular type of history written about it: not so much a history of what happened there but a history of choices that were made there. One can scroll back in time from those drawings to reflect on the circumstances of the foundation of the priory, and specifically on the decisions that were made about matters as fundamental as its monastic order and its architectural design. One can scroll back further to reflect on Geoffrey himself, on the world of his experience, and on the challenges which he faced and on the choices he made, as a settler in a relatively remote territory who was charged with the responsibility to attract other settlers.

'Colonial' Tristernagh, an idea contained in the title of this short book, conveys the sense that the priory is part of the story of Anglo-Norman colonization in Ireland. The contemporary written record, of which the charters in the register are the most important items, confirms this. The two artists recorded for us in 1779 evidence which helps us to understand that concept of colonial monasticism a little better. We are lucky that they made the trip to Tristernagh when they did.

Notes

INTRODUCTION

1 M.V. Clarke (ed.), *Register of the priory of the Blessed Virgin Mary at Tristernagh* (Dublin, 1941).

2 Brendan Scott, 'The dissolution of the religious houses in the Tudor diocese of Meath', *Archivium Hibernicum*, 59 (2005), 268. For a general discussion of Tristernagh in the context of the dissolution see Brendan Scott, *Religion and reformation on the Tudor diocese of Meath* (Dublin, 2006), passim.

3 Clarke, *Register*, pp xvi–xvii; J. Thompson, 'William Reeves and the medieval texts and manuscripts in Armagh', *Peritia*, 10 (1996), 363–80.

4 Clarke, *Register*.

5 Elizabeth Hickey, 'Some notes on Kilbixy, Tristernagh and Templecross, and the family of Piers who lived in the abbey of Tristernagh in Westmeath', *Ríocht na Midhe*, 7 (1980–1), 52–75.

6 Brian Eager, 'Tristernagh Priory: the establishment of a colonial monastic house in the Lordship of Meath (*c.*1200)' in W.J. Sheils and D. Wood (eds), *The churches, Ireland and the Irish*, Studies in Church History 25 (Oxford, 1989), pp 25–36.

7 Peter Wallace, *Ballynacarrigy, Sonna and Emper: history, heritage and community* (Athlone, 2014).

8 See, as an example, Arlene Hogan, *The priory of Llanthony Prima and Secunda in Ireland, 1172–1541* (Dublin, 2007).

9 See Tadhg O'Keeffe, *Medieval Irish buildings, 1100–1600* (Dublin, 2015).

1. THE DE COSTENTIN FAMILY AND KILBIXY

1 For de Lacy in Meath see Colin Veach, *Lordship in four realms: the Lacy family, 1166–1241* (Manchester, 2014); Rory

Masterson, *Medieval Fore, Co. Westmeath* (Dublin, 2014); T. O'Keeffe, 'Trim before 1224: new thoughts on the caput of de Lacy lordship in Ireland' in Paul Duffy, Tadhg O'Keeffe and Jean-Michel Picard (eds), *From Carrickfergus to Carcassonne: the epic deeds of Hugh de Lacy during the Albigensian crusade* (Brussels, 2017), 31–56.

2 Evelyn Mullally (ed.), *The deeds of the Normans in Ireland* (Dublin, 2002), lines 3154–5.

3 Paul MacCotter, *Medieval Ireland: territorial, political and economic divisions* (Dublin 2008), p. 199; 'The functions of the cantred in medieval Ireland', *Peritia*, 19 (2005), 310, n.5.

4 Clarke, *Register*, pp vii–viii.

5 J.T. Gilbert (ed.), *Chartularies of St Mary's Abbey, Dublin*, 2 vols (London, 1884), i, 142.

6 Clarke, *Register*, p. x, n.2.

7 W. Stubb (ed.), *Gesta Regis Henrici Secundi et Gesta Regis Ricardi Benedicti abbatis*, 2 vols (London, 1867), ii, 134.

8 G.H. Orpen, *Ireland under the Normans*, 4 vols (Oxford, 1911), i, 329, 375.

9 Brian Hodkinson, 'A summary of recent work on the Rock of Dunamase, Co. Laois' in John R. Kenyon and Kieran O'Conor (eds), *The medieval castle in Ireland and Wales* (Dublin, 2003), pp 47–8.

10 Aubrey Gwynn, 'The early history of St Thomas' Abbey, Dublin', *Journal of the Royal Society of Antiquaries of Ireland*, 84 (1954), 14.

11 G.H. Orpen, 'The castle of Raymond Le Gros at Fodredunolan', *Journal of the Royal Society of Antiquaries of Ireland*, 36 (1906), 371.

12 A.B. Scott and F.X. Martin (eds), *Expugnatia Hibernica: the conquest of Ireland by Giraldus Cambrensis* (Dublin, 1978), p. 195; A.J. Otway-Ruthven, *A history of medieval Ireland* (London, 1968), p. 75.

13 He had been a witness at the Treaty of Devizes back in 1153 (Clarke, *Register*, p. viii), so he was at least in his 60s by 1181.

14 H.S. Sweetman, *Calendar of documents relating to Ireland, 1171–1252* (London, 1875), no. 1942.

15 In the late 1320s and early 1330s Richard Costantyn and Geoffrey de Constantyn were successive tenants of the land of Ofithely, held of the manor of Dunamase by fortnightly suit to its court (A.J. Otway-Ruthven, 'Knights' fees in counties Kildare, Leix and Offaly', *Journal of the Royal Society of Antiquaries of Ireland*, 91 (1961), 177).

16 Scott and Martin, *Expugnatia Hibernica*, p. 195.

17 David Wilkins, *Concilia Magnae Britanniae et Hiberniae*, 2 vols (London, 1737), i, 547.

18 Colin Veach, 'A question of timing: Walter de Lacy's seisin of Meath 1189–94', *Proceedings of the Royal Irish Academy*, 109C (2009), 165–94.

19 'The castle of Ath-in-urchair [Ardnurcher], and the castle of Cill-Bixsighe [Kilbixy], were erected in this year' (W.M. Hennessy (ed.), *The annals of Loch Cé* (London, 1871), p. 187). The castle was strengthened during John's campaign in Ireland in 1211–12 (Oliver Davies and David B. Quinn, 'The Irish Pipe Roll of 14 John, 1211–1212', *Ulster Journal of Archaeology* 3rd ser., 4 (1941), 39).

20 The original confirmatory grant was seen by Sir James Ware; see Walter Harris, *The whole works of Sir James Ware concerning Ireland, revised and improved*, 2 vols (Dublin, 1764), ii, 198). A record of the grant, to 'Galfrid', a variant of the name Geoffrey, is preserved in British Library, Cotton MS Titus B XI, fol. 72 [33 Edw. I. 62].

21 'Onomasticon Goedelicum locorum et tribuum Hiberniae et Scotiae' [http://publish.ucc.ie/doi/locus/C].

22 Veach, *Lordship in four realms*, p. 89.

23 A.J. Otway-Ruthven, 'Knight service in Ireland', *Journal of the Royal Society of Antiquaries of Ireland*, 89 (1959), 1–15.

24 H.G. Richardson and G.O. Sayles, *The governance of medieval England* (Edinburgh, 1963), p. 60.

25 Steven G. Ellis, 'Taxation and defence in late medieval Ireland: the survival of scutage', *Journal of the Royal Society of Antiquaries of Ireland*, 107 (1977), 5–6.

26 See, for example, R. Allen Brown, *The Normans and the Norman conquest* (London, 1985), p. 190. The feudal host was an army assembled under summons by the tenants-in-chief of the crown, with each of those tenants bringing with them the knights expected from his particular land-grant.

27 Clarke, *Register*, p. 2 [Lit. 1].

28 For the functions of chambers and halls see O'Keeffe, *Medieval Irish buildings*, pp 210–17.

29 Clarke, *Register*, p. 5 [Lit. 2].

30 Clarke, *Register*, p. 3 [Lit. 1].

31 Howard B. Clarke, 'Planning and regulation in the formation of new towns and new quarters in Ireland, 1170–1641' in Anngret Simms and Howard B. Clarke (eds), *Lords and towns in medieval Europe* (Farnham, 2015), pp 21–54.

32 For a discussion of the term see John Bradley, 'Rural boroughs in medieval Ireland: nucleated or dispersed settlements?', *Ruralia*, 3 (2000), 288–93.

33 H.J. Lawlor, 'A calendar of the register of Archbishop Fleming', *Proceedings of the Royal Irish Academy*, 30 (1912–13), 131; see also Gerard A. Lee, 'The leper hospitals of the upper Shannon area', *Journal of the Old Athlone Society*, 1 (1974–5), 222–9.

34 Revd A. Cogan, *Ecclesiastical history of the diocese of Meath: ancient and modern*, 3 vols (Dublin, 1870), iii, 577.

35 NLI, MS723-4; http://downsurvey.tcd.ie/down-survey-maps.php#bm=Moygoish&c=Westmeath&p=Killbixy.

36 Aubrey Gwynn and Neville Hadcock, *Medieval religious houses: Ireland* (London, 1970), p. 351.

37 Cogan, *Ecclesiastical history of the diocese of Meath*, p. 577.

38 Newport B. White (ed.), *Extents of Irish monastic possessions, 1540–1541* (Dublin, 1943), p. 276; Sir Henry Piers, *A chorographical description of the county of Westmeath* (Dublin, 1770), p. 77.

39 Pádraig Ó Riain, *A dictionary of Irish saints* (Dublin, 2011), p. 106. See also Leo Swan, 'The early Christian ecclesiastical sites of county Westmeath' in John Bradley (ed.), *Settlement and society in medieval Ireland* (Kilkenny, 1988), p. 13.

40 T. O'Keeffe, 'The built environment of local community worship between the late eleventh and early thirteenth centuries' in Elizabeth FitzPatrick and Raymond Gillespie (eds), *The parish in medieval and early modern Ireland* (Dublin, 2006), pp 124–46.

41 Clarke, *Register*, p. 90 [Lit. IX].

42 See O'Keeffe, 'The built environment of local community worship', for a discussion.

43 Clarke, *Register*, p. 91 [Lit. X].

44 Helen M. Roe, *Medieval fonts of Meath* (Navan, 1968), p. 123.

45 Piers, *A chorographical description*, p. 77.

46 NLI, MS723–4; http://downsurvey.tcd.ie/down-survey-maps.php#bm=Moygoish&c=Westmeath&p=Killbixy.

2. THE FOUNDATION OF TRISTERNAGH PRIORY

1 Sweetman, *Calendar of documents relating to Ireland, 1171–1252*, no. 137.

2 Sweetman, *Calendar of documents relating to Ireland, 1171–1252*, no. 153.

3 Helen Perros, 'Crossing the Shannon frontier: Connacht and the Anglo-Normans, 1170–1224' in T.B. Barry, Robin Frame and Katharine Simms (eds), *Colony and frontier in medieval Ireland* (London, 1995), p. 127

4 Sweetman, *Calendar of documents relating to Ireland, 1171–1252*, nos 157, 160.

5 G.H. Orpen, 'Athlone Castle: its early history, with notes on some neighbouring castles', *Journal of the Royal Society of Antiquaries of Ireland*, 37 (1907), 257–76.

6 Sweetman, *Calendar of documents relating to Ireland, 1171–1252*, no. 612.

7 Sweetman, *Calendar of documents relating to Ireland, 1171–1252*, nos 508, 590; W.L. Warren, 'King John and Ireland' in James Lydon (ed.), *England and Ireland in the later Middle Ages* (Dublin, 1981), p. 30.

8 Thomas Finan, *Landscape and history on the medieval Irish frontier: the king's cantreds in the 13th century* (Turnhout, 2016), pp 49–51.

9 Sweetman, *Calendar of documents relating to Ireland, 1171–1252*, nos 653, 1719.

10 *Close Rolls of the reign of Henry III, 1227–31* (London, 1902), p. 171. The place is now known as Thorpe Constantine.

11 Sweetman, *Calendar of documents relating to Ireland, 1171–1252*, nos 1717, 1723, 1745.

12 Marie Thérèse Flanagan, *The transformation of the Irish church in the twelfth century* (Woodbridge, 2010).

13 Clarke, *Register*, pp 1–4 [Lit. 1], 5–6 [Lit. 2].

14 Clarke, *Register*, p. xii.

15 See, for example, J.A. Frost, *The foundation of Nostell Priory, 1109–1153* (York, 2007), p. 16; see also Dauvit Broun, 'The presence of witnesses and the writing of charters' in Dauvit Broun (ed.), *The reality behind charter diplomatic in Anglo-Norman Britain* (Glasgow 2011), pp 235–90.

16 Clarke, *Register*, pp 1–4 [Lit. 1].

17 Clarke, *Register*, p. 128.

18 Identified as a river from Sonna Demesne to Kilbixy (Clarke, *Register*, p. 130).

19 By the 1290s they had apparently purchased another canal connecting the mills at Sonna to their lands, and it ran through land that belonged to John de Tuit, and the priors needed his permission to repair it (Clarke, *Register*, pp 77–8 [Lit. LXXXXIII]).

20 Balrothery remained a key possession: Richard de Costentin paid scutage from his lands in Balrothery in 1297 (H.S. Sweetman, *Calendar of documents relating to Ireland, 1293–1301* (London, 1875), no. 442). In 1641 the Piers family, owners of Tristernagh, still owned former priory land in Balrothery (R.C. Simington (ed.), *The Civil Survey A.D. 1654–1656: vol. vii, County of Dublin* (Dublin, 1945), pp 14, 15).

21 See, for example, Clarke, *Register*, p. 82 [Lit. 1].

22 Clarke, *Register*, p. 115 [Lit. XLIX].

23 Harris, *The whole works of Sir James Ware*, ii, p. 141.

24 Clarke, *Register*, p. 89 [Lit. VIII].

25 For a discussion of Simon and his career see Rhiannon Carey Bates and Tadhg O'Keeffe, 'Colonial monasticism, the politics of patronage, and the beginnings of Gothic in Ireland: the Victorine cathedral priory of Newtown Trim, Co. Meath', *Journal of Medieval Monastic Studies*, 6 (2017), 51–76.

26 Clarke, *Register*, p. 2 [Lit. 1].

27 Clarke, *Register*, p. 89 [Lit. VIII].

28 Clarke, *Register*, p. 99 [Lit. XXIII], p. 100 [Lit. XXV], p. 103 [Lit. XXIX].

29 Daniel Brown, *Hugh de Lacy, first earl of Ulster: rising and falling in Angevin Ireland* (Woodbridge, 2016), p. 36

30 Gwynn and Hadcock, *Medieval religious houses*, pp 124–5.

31 In 1682 Sir Henry Piers noted that it 'supplieth the defect of our mother church at Kilbixy, now out of repair' (*A chorographical description*, p. 73).

32 Vincent Hurley, 'The early church in the south-west of Ireland – settlement and organization' in S.M. Pearce (ed.), *The early church in western Britain and Ireland* (Oxford, 1982), pp 297–329.

33 R. Johnson, 'A descriptive account of the decoration on the early medieval shrine known as the Corp Naomh' in T. Condit and C. Corlett (eds), *Above and beyond: essays in memory of Leo Swan* (Dublin, 2005), 303–18.

34 Sir Henry Piers noted that 'one small bell, which had the good fortune to the escape the fury and rapine of the late war' was still hanging in the church in the late 17th century (*A chorographical description*, p. 73), but this cannot have been the early medieval bell; it would have been a hand bell.

35 It might not be entirely coincidental that *Bohereennamarve* runs past a small circular mound with a narrow surrounding berm and a wide outer ditch, features that suggest that it was a ringbarrow – a burial monument – of late prehistoric date. It was described in 1840 as Crossharry Bull Ring, a name which may explain the later insertion of a corkscrew pathway to its summit.

36 White, *Extents*, p. 276.

37 B.W. O'Dwyer, *The conspiracy of Mellifont: an episode in the history of the Cistercian order in Ireland* (Dundalk, 1970).

38 We cannot be sure that the attack, the aim of which was 'to injure the English who were in it' (John O'Donovan, *Annals of the Kingdom of Ireland by the Four Masters*, 7 vols (Dublin, 1856), iii, 127), was on the ecclesiastical complex as distinct from the nearby settlement. Simon might well have desired a relocation to the more central place that was Trim, and used the attack as the pretext.

39 For what little is known see Gwynn and Hadcock, *Medieval religious houses*, p. 159.

40 O'Keeffe, *Medieval Irish buildings*, p. 159.

41 G. Constable and B. Smith (eds), *Libellus de diversis ordinibus et professionibus qui sunt in aecclesia* (Oxford, 1972). This is an account, pan-European in relevance, of how the various medieval orders of monks, canons, and hermits compared with each other, written by a regular canon in the diocese of Liège in the 1130s or 1140s.

42 Constable and Smith, *Libellus*, p. 44.

43 John Howe, *Before the Gregorian reform: the Latin church at the turn of the first millennium* (Ithaca, 2016), pp 257–61.

44 Constable and Smith, *Libellus*, pp 56, 92.

45 P.J. Dunning, 'The Arroasian order in medieval Ireland', *Irish Historical Studies*, 4 (1945), 297–315.

46 However, its church was later recorded as a parish church (White, *Extents*, p. 276).

47 Richard W. Pfaff, *The liturgy in medieval England: a history* (Cambridge, 2009), p. 284.

48 Gwynn and Hadcock, *Medieval religious houses*, p. 152.

49 Although there may have been Irish-born canons, no native lords made grants to the priory, and there was only ever one prior of native descent, William Ó Faelain, 1483–85. The list of Tristernagh's priors up to the end of the 15th century can be reconstructed principally from papal sources, but not all the dates are known and there may be gaps in the sequence: Henry, before 1224; Richard de Hamme before 1235; Thomas […], 1248; William de Clastonia, 1262; Richard […], 1273/4; Richard de Sonnagh, 1281; Richard Comyn, [?]; William […], 1286–?1291; Nicholas Frend, 1291; John Hacket, 1296/7; Richard […], 1318; A[…] de C[…] ?1318; Richard de Drogheda, 1364; John Hill, 1387; […]; Richard Ro[u]we, *c.*1401–11; Richard Hill, 1411; William Warynge, 1412–23; John Warynge, 1427; Walter Noulla [Nonlla], *c.*1439–49; Geoffrey de la Mare [Lemara], 1449–67/8; Simon Nugent, before 1483; William Ó Faelain 1483–85; Richard Tuit, 1485–1502/3; Maurive Dalton, 1492 (*Calendar of entries in the papal registers relating to Great Britain and Ireland*, 14 vols (London 1893–1960), passim; Clarke, *Register*, p. xxiii).

50 John T. Gilbert (ed.), *Register of the abbey of St Thomas, Dublin* (London, 1889), pp 241–2.

51 Gwynn and Hadcock, *Medieval religious houses*, p. 163.

52 Clarke, *Register*, pp 34–5 [Lit. XXXVII].

53 Charles McNeill (ed.), *Calendar of Archbishop Alen's register, c.1172–1534* (Dublin, 1950), pp 33, 59.

54 Clarke, Register, pp 19–20 [Lit. XVIII], 35 [XXXVIII], 39 [Lit. XLIIII], 44 [Lit. LI].

55 Clarke, *Register*, pp 27 [Lit. XXIX], 29 [Lit. XXXII], 41 [Lit. XLVII].

56 Five carucates in Grange and ten in *Dunbanan* or *Donbanon* (Clarke, *Register*, pp 33–4 [Lit. XXXVI] and 38–9 [Lit. XLIII].

57 See, for example, Clarke, *Register*, p. 45 [Lit. LI].

58 Clarke, *Register*, p. 7 [Lit. IIII].

59 W.H. Bliss and J.A. Twemlow (eds), *Calendar of papal registers relating to Great Britain and Ireland*, vol. 6, *1404–1415* (London, 1904), p. 31.

60 Bliss and Twemlow, *Calendar of papal registers, 1404–1415*, p. 157.

61 Ecclesiastical courts had no juries, so all proceedings were written down – in 'cause' papers – for the benefit of the presiding judge. See Richard H. Helmholz, 'Canonical defamation in medieval England,' *American Journal of Legal History*, 255 (1971), 255–68.

62 Bliss and Twemlow, *Calendar of papal registers, 1404–1415*, p. 276.

63 E.B. Fitzmaurice and A.G. Little, *Materials for the history of the Franciscan province in Ireland* (Manchester, 1920), pp 104–5.

3. A COLONIAL ARCHITECTURE: GOTHIC TRISTERNAGH

1 Peter Harbison, *Our treasure of antiquities: Beranger and Bigari's antiquarian sketching tour of Connacht in 1779* (Bray, 2002), pp 1–5.

2 Harbison, *Our treasure of antiquities*, p. 40.

3 His name is rendered here following the spelling in John Burke, *A general and heraldic dictionary of the peerage and baronetage of the British empire*, 3 vols (London, 1830), iii, 604. See this source for the following brief history of the Piers family, and Pedigree of Piers of Tristernagh, Co. Westmeath, Barts.,

*c.*1500–1815 (NLI Genealogical Office: MS 112, pp 20–1).

4 The O'Neills and the Mageoghegans attacked Kilbixy in 1430 and 1450 respectively (O'Donovan, *Annals of the Kingdom of Ireland by the Four Masters*, iv, 879, 971).

5 For the history of the Piers family see Clarke, *Register*, pp xiv–xvi; Hickey, 'Some notes on Kilbixy, Tristernagh and Templecross'.

6 Clarke, *Register*, p. xvii, incorrectly claims that Ware's son, Robert, was married to the daughter of Sir Henry.

7 G.E. Cokayne, *The complete peerage of England, Scotland, Ireland, Great Britain and the United Kingdom, extant, extinct or dormant*, 8 vols (London, 1887–98), i, 444.

8 In the late Georgian period it was, reputedly, the model for Maria Edgeworth's Castle Rackrent (Paul Walsh, *The placenames of Westmeath* (Dublin, 1915), p. 39).

9 J.N. Brewer, *The beauties of Ireland*, 2 vols (London, 1826), ii, 239.

10 It has been dated to the 17th century (Donal O'Brien, *The houses and landed families of Westmeath* (Athlone, 2014), p. 212), but it is 18th century in date, and was re-panelled on the inside in, probably, the early 19th century.

11 James Woods, *Annals of Westmeath. Ancient and modern* (Dublin, 1907), pp 309–10.

12 Brewer, *The beauties of Ireland*, ii, 239.

13 Peter Harbison, 'Gabriel Beranger' in James McGuire and James Quinn (eds), *Dictionary of Irish biography* (Cambridge, 2009).

14 Harbison, *Our treasure of antiquities*, p. 8.

15 Harbison, *Our treasure of antiquities*, p. 10.

16 Harbison, *Our treasure of antiquities*, p. 10.

17 NLI, 2122 TX(3), p. 29, p. 30 respectively.

18 Francis Grose, *The antiquities of Ireland*, 2 vols (London, 1791), ii, 50–1.

19 NLI, MS 671.

20 My thanks to Mr Andrew Roohan for allowing me access to the site.

21 For the claustral plan in Augustinian monasteries in Ireland see Tadhg O'Keeffe, 'Augustinian regular canons in twelfth- and thirteenth-century Ireland: history, architecture and identity' in

Janet Burton and Karen Stober (eds), *The regular canons in the medieval British Isles* (Brussels, 2012), pp 460–74.

22 Tadhg O'Keeffe, *An Anglo-Norman monastery: Bridgetown Priory and the architecture of the Augustinian canons regular in Ireland* (Kinsale, 1999).

23 P. Fergusson, 'The refectory at Easby Abbey: form and iconography', *Art Bulletin,* 71 (1989), 334–51.

24 Elizabeth Hickey suggested that they were playing a known game in which the object tied to the pole is a cake and is the prize ('Some notes on Kilbixy, Tristernagh and Templecross', 70).

25 See also Thomas Cromwell, *Excursions through Ireland: province of Leinster* (London, 1820), p. 168.

26 Tadhg O'Keeffe, 'The design of the early 13th-century cathedral church of Newtown Trim, Co. Meath', *Ríocht na Midhe,* 29 (2018), 14–26.

27 O'Keeffe, *Medieval Irish buildings*, pp 117–20.

28 O'Keeffe, 'Newtown Trim'.

29 Tadhg O'Keeffe, 'A cryptic puzzle from medieval Dublin', *Archaeology Ireland,* 31:2 (2017), 39–43.

30 Henry Summerson and Stuart Harrison, *Lanercost Priory, Cumbria: a survey and documentary history* (Kendal, 2000), p. 179.

31 Though based on surviving fabric, the design of Ferns is speculative: see Tadhg O'Keeffe and Rhiannon Carey Bates, 'The abbey and cathedral of Ferns, 1111–1253' in Ian Doyle and Bernard Browne (eds), *Medieval Wexford: essays in memory of Billy Colfer* (Dublin, 2016), pp 73–96.

32 Roger Stalley, *The Cistercian monasteries of Ireland* (New Haven, 1987), pp 96–7.

33 Piers, *A chorographical description*, p. 71.

34 Martin Heale, *The dependent priories of medieval English monasteries* (Woodbridge, 2004), pp 53–4, 104.

35 Summerson and Harrison, *Lanercost Priory*. The same form is found in mid-13th-century Brechin Cathedral, confirming its northern British character. At Lanercost the aisle was added to solve a problem of access to the choir which had previously been solved by having

a single bay tucked into the return of the nave and the north transept. There may have been a similar bay in the same position at Newtown Trim, but it was never developed into an aisle because of the failure of that church to become the accepted cathedral church of the diocese (see Carey Bates and O'Keeffe, 'The Victorine cathedral priory of Newtown Trim').

36 O'Keeffe, *Medieval Irish buildings*, p 80.

37 Jill A. Franklin, 'Augustinian and other canons' churches in Romanesque Europe: the significance of the aisleless cruciform plan' in J.A. Franklin, T.A. Heslop and C. Stevenson (eds), *Architecture and interpretation: essays for Eric Fernie* (Woodbridge, 2012), pp 8–98. An aisle was added early in the 13th century to the late 12th-century church in Kells Priory, Co. Kilkenny (Miriam Clyne, *Kells priory, Co. Kilkenny: archaeological excavations by T. Fanning & M. Clyne* (Dublin, 2007), p. 99). For a discussion of the Irish evidence see T. O'Keeffe, 'Transeptal churches of the regular canons in Ireland', in Martin Browne and Colmán Ó Clabaigh (eds), *Augustinian canons and canoness in Ireland* (Dublin, 2019), *forthcoming*.

38 Peter Draper, *The formation of English Gothic: architecture and identity, 1150–1250* (New Haven, 2006).

39 Carey Bates and O'Keeffe, 'Colonial monasticism'; O'Keeffe, 'A cryptic puzzle'.

40 Tadhg O'Keeffe, 'Wheels of words, networks of knowledge: Romanesque scholarship and Cormac's Chapel' in Damian Bracken and Dagmar Ó Riain-Raedel (eds), *Ireland and Europe in the twelfth century: reform and renewal* (Dublin, 2006), pp 257–69.

CONCLUSION

1 Brewer, *The beauties of Ireland*, ii, 238–9.

2 Clarke, *Register*, p. 89 [Lit. VIII].

3 RIA/Upton papers/22, 5 [undated]; 23 (57) [18 August, 1915; 6 November, 1916].